THE NEW
Christian Charm
COURSE
TEACHER BOOK

EMILY HUNTER
JODY CAPEHART
ANGELA CARNATHAN
WITH AMY KENDRICK PIERSON

HARVEST HOUSE PUBLISHERS

EUGENE, OREGON

Angela Carnathan photo © Harold Carnathan

Jody Capehart photo © C. David Edmonson

Cover photos © iStockphoto

Cover by Dugan Design Group, Bloomington, Minnesota

NEW CHRISTIAN CHARM COURSE (TEACHER)
Copyright © 2009 Emily Hunter, Jody Capehart, and Angela Carnathan
Published by Harvest House Publishers
Eugene, Oregon 97402
www.harvesthousepublishers.com

ISBN 978-0-7369-2577-8

Printed in the United States of America

09 10 11 12 13 14 15 16 17 / VP-KB / 10 9 8 7 6 5 4 3 2 1

*To the teen girls who want to know more about Christ
and also to become delightful young women who enjoy life.
We're delighted you're taking this journey.*

*To the women who lovingly care for teens girls and
want to help them discover who they are in Christ
and experience all He offers here on earth and for eternity.*

*May the Lord bless your willingness
to teach…to learn…to live life
as fully as possible.*

Jody's Acknowledgments

When Bob Hawkins Jr., president of Harvest House Publishers, asked me to lead the updating of the *New Christian Charm Course*, I was honored. Emily Hunter's *Christian Charm Course* embodied my core convictions and desire to help teen girls grow in Christ and in confidence. God's hand "connected the dots" to bring this project together so girls can discover how exciting life in Christ can be. Many people made this project possible:

✿ It's been a joy to work closely with my daughter, Angela.

✿ Amy Kendrick Pierson and Mona Corwin provided writing, valuable insights, prayers, friendship, godly wisdom, and personal support.

✿ Karen Bannis and Patty Couture provided practical advice and support.

✿ The precious 8th grade girls at Legacy Christian Academy were a delightful part of this project. As my coauthors and I worked through the charm course lessons, I taught them to "my girls" each week. Girls, you provided wonderful advice. May you continue to grow in Christlike character, confidence, and charm. I love and appreciate each of you. A special thanks to Morgan Anderson, Adrienne Baker, Ann Byrd, Lexy Crane, Alyssa Dunlap, Alyssa Hollowell, Rachel Hooker, Maddie Keen, Allie Lebos, Cindy Lin, Katelyn Mason, Melisa Meeks, Sarah Miller, Fernanda Garcia-Olivares, Abby Paxton, Katelyn Pennington, Audrey Reese, Elizabeth Wallbillich, Alexandra Walsh, Sarah Weimer, Kaitlyn York, and Emily Zenthoefer.

✿ The Harvest House family, who is a joy to work with on every level. A special thanks to Bob Hawkins Jr. and LaRae Weikert for their gifts of leadership and friendship; Carolyn McCready for her godly wisdom, editing insights, and faithful heart of love; Barb Gordon for her editing gifts and willingness to *go the extra mile* with a kind heart; and Pat Mathis, who is always cheerful and has a "can do" spirit!

✿ Thank you, dear family members, including my incredibly supportive husband, Paul, and faithful friends who provided prayer support. I wish there was space to acknowledge each of you personally. My heart overflows with love and gratitude for each of you.

Angela's Acknowledgments

To my husband, Harold, and my boys Keagan and Hudson—who love and support me. You are my pride and joy, and I can't imagine life without you. Also to my mom, who has always been an amazing inspiration to me. She has always been there to guide, encourage, and love me through my own teenage years and now as a mother myself. Thank you and I love you!

Amy's Acknowledgments

To my sweet new hubby, Kyle, and to my mom, grandmother, Aunt Shan, Aunt Sheila, Mrs. Gina, and all the sweet saints at Salem Heights who modeled what it looked like to be a Christian lady from the inside out.

Contents

A Letter to Teachers

Dear Teachers,

As mentors, we're going to be teaching girls the art of Christian charm, which reflects *Christlike character, changed hearts, commitment, confidence,* and *social graces.* At the core of the *New Christian Charm Course* is a sincere faith in Jesus. Beauty radiates from within, from believing and living for Jesus. We can teach girls how to look their best, but Jesus provides the special glow that creates arresting loveliness.

To get the most out of this material, we suggest focusing on these four "P's":

- ✿ *Purpose.* To help you focus, each lesson includes a clearly stated purpose.

- ✿ *Prayer.* Pray for your preparation time, and begin each class with prayer. Provide 3 x 5 colored note cards and an attractive "Confidential Prayer Requests" container. Explain that the girls can share their prayer requests, and only you will read them and pray for them. Before class, place the cards and container in an easily seen but unobtrusive place.

- ✿ *Ponder the Scriptures.* Memorize the five core *Christian Charm Course* verses. You'll be helping the girls memorize them as well. In class periodically review the verses and have the girls recite them. These verses are in the "Connecting with Christ" section, so they're easy to find and review.

- ✿ *Preparation.* Each lesson includes a list of supplies. Many chapters have descriptions of two girls for role-playing to highlight the main point in a fun way.

We offer these suggestions to help you make this course interesting, meaningful, and clear.

Be familiar with the material. Review each lesson ahead of time so you'll know the lesson, gather the equipment and resources required for the lesson, and have a general plan to present the information. Although we've provided suggestions on what to say, please feel free to let your personality and teaching style shine by "making the material your own."

Promote a peaceful environment: Counter the harried and hectic world the girls live in by creating an atmosphere of peaceful interaction. Why not play classical music in the background, use lamps for soft lighting, and place beautiful flowers around? Model charm by dressing with class. With today's casual attire, it may be unrealistic to expect the girls to dress in a certain way. However, we've found that girls' actions and attitudes are influenced by how they dress. Hopefully by the end of this course their clothing will be appropriate for representatives of Jesus.

Be ready and greet the girls when they arrive. Have the environment prepared and ready. Stand by the door and greet each girl by name, shaking her hand, looking into her eyes with warmth, and making her feel special and welcome. Encourage her to greet you the same way.

We know you're going to be blessed beyond measure as you get to know "your" girls better and help them become the young women God created them to be.

Your partners in Christ,

Emily, Jody, Angela, and Amy

Connecting with Christ

In each class go over one of these scriptures and discuss the characteristics. Interact with the girls to find out what they think the words mean. You may be surprised to find out how they interpret the words. Invite discussion, encouraging each person to share. Avoid being negative. If someone shares something you disagree with, simply say, "That's interesting. Thank you. Does anyone else want to share?"

Note: The student workbook has goal and scripture only.

1. *Christlike character:* This is the overall theme.

    Finally, [sisters], whatever is true, whatever is noble, whatever is right, whatever is pure, whatever is lovely, whatever is admirable—if anything is excellent or praiseworthy—think about such things (Philippians 4:8).

2. *Changed hearts:* We are changing and growing through Christ.

    If anyone is in Christ, he is a new creation, the old has gone, the new has come! (2 Corinthians 5:17).

3. *Committed:* We are dedicated to the cause of Christ, which includes serving others.

    Whatever you do, work at it with all your heart, as working for the Lord, not for men, since you know that you will receive an inheritance from the Lord as a reward. It is the Lord Christ you are serving (Colossians 3:24).

4. *Confident:* We are strong and courageous in the Lord.

> *I can do everything through him who gives me strength* (Philippians 4:13).

5. *Charming:* We attract others to Christ because they see a difference in us, and that difference is our gentle spirit and love for one another.

> *As God's chosen people, holy and dearly loved, clothe yourselves with compassion, kindness, humility, gentleness and patience. Bear with each other and forgive whatever grievances you may have against one another. Forgive as the Lord forgave you. And over all these virtues put on love, which binds them all together in perfect unity* (Colossians 3:12-14).

Within and Without

Your Life in Christ

Purpose

To help the girls see they are who God designed them to be. Also to guide them to seeing their true identities in Christ.

Note: You may have to use several class times to complete the first chapter.

Prayer

Lord, help me as I prepare to teach this charm course. I want to be supportive and encouraging as I work with the girls. Show me how to love them with Your love and teach them what You want them to know. In Your name I pray. Amen.

Ponder

"If anyone is in Christ, he is a new creation; the old has gone, the new has come!" (2 Corinthians 5:17).

Prepare

* digital cameras
* full-length mirror
* enough Bibles and pencils for the girls to share
* sign-up sheet for contact information

We suggest you establish a pleasant, supportive atmosphere by greeting each girl when they come in. You can…

🌸 be calmly standing at the door

🌸 shake each girl's hand firmly, make eye contact, and tell her you're glad she's here

🌸 ask her to find a place and sit down

Ask two girls ahead of time to role-play *Slouched Sally* and *Poised Petunia*. Tell them to "ham it up" by exaggerating the characteristics of the two girls.

Slouched Sally sits in a chair slumped low. Her legs are sprawled out, and her heels are on the floor with her toes sticking up. Her back is curved as she slants a bit sideways. She has her arms crossed.

Poised Petunia sits in a chair with her back straight but relaxed. She has her knees together, and her legs are angled a little to the side. Her feet are resting on the floor. Her arms are by her sides; her hands rest in her lap.

Welcome to Your New Christian Charm Course

Note: To help you, we've provided sample or suggested teacher dialogue. This material is indented and in quote marks.

"Welcome to your Christian charm course! We're going on an amazing adventure to find out how best to present ourselves to people every day…and to discover who we are on the inside, in Christ.

"But before we begin, let's start with prayer."

Pray for the class, for your teaching, for hearts to be open to what God wants each person to learn. Thank God for bringing everyone to class and for blessing the class time.

"The first thing we want to do is get your contact information. I'm going to pass around a registration form you can fill out while we're getting started. I'm also going to pass out the workbooks we'll be using."

On the signup sheet have places for the girls to write *and* print their names, their contact phone numbers, their home addresses, and their ages.

"A charm course may seem a bit old-fashioned, but the principles of good manners are everlasting. We're going to explore how to cultivate hearts dedicated to God, Christlike character, confidence, commitment, integrity, and, yes, even charm. We want to please God and represent Him well."

Note: At first the girls may groan and roll their eyes at the idea of learning about charm, but we assure you, in time they'll *love* this class. So stay calm, don't lecture, and be patient. Give them time. This is *counterculture*, and it isn't "modern" to like something like this. They will come around. We haven't had a group yet who didn't in due time. Breathe…smile…have faith.

A good way to start is to share something interesting and personal about good manners you've learned from life that the girls can relate to. If you're transparent, they will understand that this class is a *safe* place where honesty is encouraged and no one has to be perfect because of the saving grace of Jesus.

"Turn to the beginning of your workbook and find the page called 'Connecting with Christ.' Write your name under the picture of the girl. She represents you.

"As we go through this charm course, we're going to memorize these five verses. By having God's Word in our minds and hearts, we can call on His wisdom when life isn't going as well as we hoped. We can also use the verses as encouragements to grow spiritually every day so we will please God.

"Let's read the first verse, Philippians 4:8, together:

> " *'Finally, [sisters], whatever is true, whatever is noble, whatever is right, whatever is pure, whatever is lovely, whatever is admirable—if anything is excellent or praiseworthy—think about such things.'*

"Isn't this a great reminder? Read this verse every day and memorize it for our next class.

"Okay, now we're going to look at ways to make our outer appearance more appealing. You may think it a bit odd, but the first place we start is with our hearts. Who we are on the inside is revealed by our outside. For instance, when we're feeling confident and loving, we're usually smiling and exhibiting a joyful attitude. And how do we feel confident and loving? By knowing the heart of Christ. He is love. He gives us the ability to be continually joyful. In a world that thinks the three most important people in the world are 'me, myself, and I,' we need to change our thinking to 'Jesus first, then others, and then me.' That's the biblical order. Did you notice what the initials spell? Jesus, Others, You:

J Jesus
O Others
Y You

"It's not easy, but with the Lord's help we can do it! Even though we're looking at ourselves during this course, we are doing so in the spirit of developing our *inner* selves so that our *outer* beauty shines brighter. Inner beauty comes from knowing Jesus.

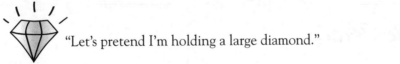 "Let's pretend I'm holding a large diamond."

Pretend to admire a large diamond in your hand.

"Look at this beautiful rock. It's extremely valuable. That is what each of you are. You are valuable, and you were purchased by God with His Son, Jesus. He sees you as a lovely diamond. And just as it took time and energy to create this diamond, it's going to take us time and energy to look and be our best.

"For the outer us, we're going to look at posture, hair, nails, clothes, and makeup to find ways to accent our positives. For the inner us, we're going to find ways to polish the true diamond in us—our lives in Jesus Christ. We'll learn how to get our hearts right so we'll shine and people will wonder, *What does she have? Where did she get it? I want it!"*

We Are Fearfully and Wonderfully Made

"Do you know that each one of you is beautiful? After all, God created you! Let's read Psalm 139:13-14 together: '*For you created my inmost being; you knit me together in my mother's womb. I praise you because I am fearfully and wonderfully made; your works are wonderful, I know that full well.*'"

"Are you happy with the way God made you? So many girls have image problems. Do you compare yourself with others? Are you trying to live up to what the world says you *should* be? Or what your friends want you to be? Or what your family says you need to be? Let me introduce you to two girls."

Have the two girls you asked to play *Slouched Sally* and *Poised Petunia* come to the front of the class and sit down.

"The first girl is Sally. Notice how she sits in a chair. She's slumped low. Her legs are sprawled out. Her heels are on the floor with her toes sticking up. Her back is curved as she slouches a bit sideways. She has her arms crossed. Let's call her *Slouched Sally*.

"The second girl is *Poised Petunia*. Notice how she sits in a chair. Her back is straight but relaxed. She has her knees together, and her legs are angled a little to the side. Her feet are resting on the floor. Her arms are by her sides; her hands rest in her lap.

"If you were choosing someone to work on a committee, which one of these girls would you choose? Or if you were going to pick someone to speak at an assembly, which girl would it be? Why?"

"Doesn't Slouched Sally look uninterested in what's going on? She doesn't look energized or eager. Poised Petunia, on the other hand, looks confident, relaxed, and alert.

"How about you? What do people see when they look at you?"

Before and After Pictures

"It's picture time!"

"Before" and "after" pictures add interest to the class and will help the girls see what improvements and changes they've made throughout the charm course. To get set up for this activity, here are a few suggestions.

✿ If there is a woman in your church or social group who has photography experience, why not see if she would like to help…or even head up this project?

❀ Digital cameras let you know right away if the picture turned out.

❀ Select a plain wall for the background.

❀ Put a piece of paper on the floor for the girls to stand on. This will help make all the photos uniform and easy to compare with the "after" pictures.

❀ Write down the distance between the camera and the subject, the distance between the subject and the wall, and the zoom used. You'll be duplicating these conditions when you take the "after" pictures in chapter 10.

❀ Take full body shots, including feet.

❀ Have two copies of each photo made or printed. Give one to each girl to put in her workbook. Keep the second set in case a few girls lose theirs.

Phase 1

For the first shot, ask the girls to stand how they usually do when they're comfortable. Don't give them any more guidance than that. Take full body shots.

If you can print the photos right away, go ahead. If not, have them ready for the next class.

Phase 2

Hand out the "before" photos.

Ask the girls how they felt about getting their pictures taken and what they think about their photos. Remind them not to critique their build, clothes, or hairstyle. Right now the focus is on presenting themselves in the best way possible.

 "Girls, did you feel confident as you posed for your 'before' picture? Or did you feel awkward and uneasy? Were you wondering what to do with your hands and feet?"

"Turn to 'Posing Points' in your workbooks. Under each area there are spaces where you can write ways to look your best as we go over them.

"Models are trained how to pose. Let's learn a few 'tricks of the trade' before we start phase 2 of our 'before' pictures. These tips will help you look your best all the time. Are you ready?"

Note: Student workbook doesn't include bulleted information in this section. As you share each item, have them write it down in their workbooks.

Check Your Posture

✿ sit up or stand up straight

✿ strive for a natural pose

✿ be poised and relaxed, not tense and tight

Check Your Body Profile

✿ professional photographers always pose subjects at angles

✿ few people look good with straight-on shots...not even models

✿ find your "best" angle (decide which side you want featured—your right or left)

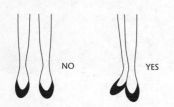

Check Your Feet

✿ keep one foot pointed toward the camera and the other slightly behind at a 45-degree angle

✿ allow your weight to rest on the foot which is behind

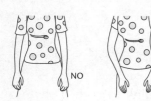

Check Your Hands

✿ don't hang your arms and hands straight down, dangling from your body

✿ curve your hands in toward the body slightly

✿ if you feel awkward, hold something in your hands

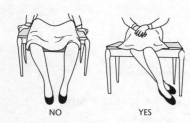

Check Your Legs

✿ although shoulders and head may be turned toward the camera, if sitting, keep your legs slanted to one side, ankles together and knees together

✿ do not point your legs toward the camera or sprawl them

✿ remember, in pictures, whatever projects toward the camera will appear larger and distorted in relation to the rest of your body

Check Your Facial Expression

✿ practice in front of the mirror so you can decide your most flattering view/side and automatically show it

✿ choose which is more becoming to you—a broad smile or a soft smile

✿ saying the word "cheese" is an old trick that helps get the proper lip formation for a "Mona Lisa" smile

Set up the picture-taking area exactly like you did for the first "before" pictures. Take pictures of each girl, making sure you get their heads down to their toes in the shots.

Have the girls practice posing while the others are getting pictures taken. They can use their cell phone cameras to take pictures of each other posing to make this fun.

If you can, immediately print two sets of photos and pass out one set. Keep one set in case some of the girls lose their photo.

"Compare your 'before' picture with your 'after' picture. Do you like the second one better? Most of you probably do. Just a few posing tips can make a big difference in how others perceive you. Amazing, how those few little tips make a big difference in how you look. Let's put both pictures under 'before' in your workbook. In chapter 10, we'll be taking another picture to show what progress we've made. You're going to look even better!"

Reflecting Christ

"Is our 'new look' complete? Your workbook quotes 1 Samuel 16:7: *'Man looks at the outward appearance, but the LORD looks at the heart.'* So even though we can make improvements to our 'outside,' if our inside is still messed up and dirty, it will alter our outside presentation.

"How can we bring about a clean heart? Is there something we can do to create a 'new look' inside? Are there pointers to fixing our inside? No! Ephesians 2:8-9 says, *'It is by grace you have been saved, through faith—and this not from yourselves, it is the gift of God—not by works, so that no one can boast.'* We do nothing to deserve God's love and favor. We don't work to earn it. We simply receive it (John 1:12). It comes as a gift, and the tag reads, 'With love to you from your heavenly Father' (see John 3:16).

"The moment we accept Christ—God's priceless gift—a miracle takes place. We are 'born again' into God's family! We receive new hearts and new natures. We are brand-new people in Christ.

"We gain a new glow, a new look because the Holy Spirit now lives within us. And the more we surrender to His control, the more He transforms us from within, filling us with joy and peace in Christ. When our hearts have found peace, a new gentleness is revealed, a lovely radiance—the light of His glory—shines through.

"So as we work on our 'outer' selves, we also want to be growing in Christ so our inner selves will add God's special touch to our outside. Then we'll truly be charming!"

Share the Gospel Message

If you have a group of girls you feel confident already believe in Jesus and know about His great sacrifice and what it means, you can skip this part. If you have one or two girls you want to share the gospel with, consider doing this one-on-one in a different setting. Of course, it never hurts to go over the basics of salvation with people to make sure they understand who Jesus is.

As you know, there are many ways to share the gospel. If you have a way you are comfortable with, use that method. Otherwise, Child Evangelism Fellowship has excellent material, as does the Navigators and other ministries. The girls' workbook includes a gospel message you can use, but feel free to augment it if you'd like. This section is called "How Do We Get This 'New Look'?" in the workbook.

 "In your workbook there are four statements that many teenagers—and adults!—say. Let's read them aloud and talk about them. Then I'll provide a scripture reference you can write down so you will have them handy if you have these questions or your friends do."

 Have the girls look up and read the scripture. Ask someone to read it aloud and then discuss it. (*Note:* The scripture portion is not in the student workbook.)

✿ "I just don't get it. The Bible is confusing. Why does God call me a sinner when I'm doing the best I can?"

> *The man without the Spirit does not accept the things that come from the Spirit of God, for they are foolishness to him, and he cannot understand them, because they are spiritually discerned* (1 Corinthians 2:14).

✿ "I'm trying to be better, but I keep messing up. It's really nobody's business but mine anyway."

> *All of us have become like one who is unclean, and all our righteous acts are like filthy rags* (Isaiah 64:6).

✿ "I don't understand why I'm not happier. I buy new things and have good friends. I'm happy for a while, but the good feeling goes away."

> *Then [Jesus] said to them, "Watch out! Be on your guard against all kinds of greed; a man's life does not consist in the abundance of his possessions"* (Luke 12:15).

✿ "Why do I feel so empty inside? What is wrong with me?"

> *Now this is eternal life: that they may know you, the only true God, and Jesus Christ, whom you have sent* (John 17:3).

After the girls read about how life has changed after accepting Jesus, share these scriptures to help them understand the transformation that takes place.

❀ "Everything has changed."

> *For God, who said, "Let light shine out of darkness," made his light shine in our hearts to give us the light of the knowledge of the glory of God in the face of Christ (2 Corinthians 4:6).*

❀ "My perspectives are changing."

> *You were taught, with regard to your former way of life, to put off your old self, which is being corrupted by its deceitful desires; to be made new in the attitude of your minds; and to put on the new self, created to be like God in true righteousness and holiness (Ephesians 4:22-24).*

❀ "I feel new power and strength in me."

> *I can do everything through him who gives me strength (Philippians 4:13).*

❀ "When Christians said the Holy Spirit helps people do what's right it never made sense."

> *No temptation has seized you except what is common to man. And God is faithful; he will not let you be tempted beyond what you can bear. But when you are tempted, he will also provide a way out so that you can stand up under it (1 Corinthians 10:13).*

❀ "I didn't see how God could love me as much as they said He did."

> *Dear friends, let us love one another, for love comes from God. Everyone who loves has been born of God and knows God (1 John 4:7-8).*

Note: Under "How Can I Become a Christian?" the student workbook explains what it means to be saved and offers a prayer of salvation.

Write from Your Heart

"Write from Your Heart" gives the girls an opportunity to journal about what they hope to accomplish. It helps them explore what you've been sharing and what they've been learning in the workbook. You can have them answer the questions in their workbooks in class or do them at home.

2

Balanced Beauty
Diet, Exercise, and You

Purpose

To help girls see the importance of taking care of their physical bodies as temples of the Holy Spirit.

Prayer

Gracious heavenly Father, help me pass on to the girls the amazing truth that the bodies You've given them are wonderful and unique. May they begin to capture the wonder of You and how the Holy Spirit resides in them. In Your Son's name I pray. Amen.

Ponder

"Do you not know that your body is a temple of the Holy Spirit, who is in you, whom you have received from God? You are not your own; you were bought at a price. Therefore honor God with your body" (1 Corinthians 6:19-20).

Preparation

❀ bring a change of clothing for demonstrating exercises or have someone come in to demonstrate the exercises

❀ a small set of weights (optional)

❀ an exercise ball (optional)

❀ 2 or 3 candy bars, bags of chips, junk food, a soda

❀ an apple, some carrots, nuts, healthy food

❀ water bottle with water

❀ Ask two girls to role-play *Lazy Leena* and *Energetic Edna*.

> *Lazy Leena* is tired and dragging. She finds it hard to move. She yawns a lot and stretches her legs and arms. She's carrying and eating and drinking junk food and a soda.

> *Energetic Edna* is happy, cheerful, energetic. She's carrying and eating and drinking healthy food and bottled water. She's athletic.

Vitality Is Essential

"Welcome! Let's start our time together with prayer."

Pray for the class, for your teaching, for hearts to be open to what God wants everyone to learn. Thank God for bringing everyone to class.

"Who would like to share the memory verse from the last class—Philippians 4:8?"

> *Finally, [sisters], whatever is true, whatever is noble, whatever is right, whatever is pure, whatever is lovely, whatever is admirable—if anything is excellent or praiseworthy—think about such things.*

"Does anyone else want to give it a try?"

[Pause.]

"Thank you, girls. Now I'd like to introduce two girls that most of you can probably relate to."

Have the two girls go out of the classroom and enter playing their parts when you say their "acting" names.

"The first girl is very tired and dragging. She's finding it hard to even move. She yawns a lot and stretches her legs and arms. We'll call her *Lazy Leena*. She's constantly eating food with a lot of fat and a lot of sugar. And she's never without a soft drink. You won't be surprised that she's decided to skip exercising today. She's just too tired and doesn't feel like exerting energy.

"The next girl is quite a contrast. *Energetic Edna* is ready to go. She's feeling great and has a smile and greeting for everyone. There's a lift in her steps and a lilt in her voice. She's eating quick energy foods that are nutritious. She's ready to help out wherever she's needed and will be a vital part of the softball game she's playing in after school."

If you'd like you can have a more thorough discussion on the differences between Lazy Leena and Energtic Edna.

 "Life can be so exciting and fulfilling! We want to have enough energy and brainpower to know what's going on and actively participate. How we take care of ourselves physically also communicates that we take care of what God has given us, which also implies we'll take care of what people give us or do what we're asked to do with zest and thoughtfulness.

"Now, turn to chapter 2 in your workbooks and read the first section."

You can have the girls take turns reading paragraphs or quickly review the material.

Vitality Comes with a Price Tag

 "When we hear the word 'discipline,' we automatically think of punishment. But discipline also means having and exercising self-control for our benefit and for those around us. In what areas do you practice self-discipline today? What are the results? Are there areas you need to have more discipline?"

Running the Race

 "Let's say we've decided to become runners. In fact, we're going to tackle a marathon, which is a 26-mile race. What will we need to do to prepare?"

Let the girls come up with four or five needed things, from training to equipment.

"Are you saying it wouldn't be enough to just decide to do it? Having enthusiasm, a 'can do' attitude, and praying about it won't make us successful?"

As you share the following information, the girls are asked to write down the definitions of "discipline" and "self-discipline" in their workbooks.

"You're right. We would need to train. And that's a biblical principle too! God's Word says, *'No discipline seems pleasant at the time, but painful. Later on, however, it produces a harvest of righteousness and peace for those who have been trained by it'* (Hebrews 12:11). Training is important. It develops in us the discipline necessary to get where we want to go. A good definition of 'discipline' is 'being able to do what needs to be done when it needs to be done.' 'Self-discipline' is 'doing a task even when we don't feel like doing it.' We don't 'feel' our way to success; we take action to be successful."

Does All of This Really Matter?

 "Do you think God cares about whether we keep ourselves healthy or not?"

[Pause.]

"If He does care, why do you think He does?"

[Pause.]

"What difference will being and staying healthy make in your Christian walk?"

[Pause.]

"The Bible says, *'Don't you know that you yourselves are God's temple and that God's Spirit lives in you? If anyone destroys God's temple, God will destroy him; for God's temple is sacred, and you are that temple'* (1 Corinthians 3:16-17). That's pretty powerful, isn't it! So yes, it's very important that we take care of our bodies. And the two most important ways to do that are eating a healthy diet and exercising regularly and consistently."

Physically Whole...Inside and Out

"What's the difference between 'junk food' and 'healthy food'?"

Emotionally Whole...Inside and Out

"What is stress? It's 'when body or mental tension results from factors that cause our equilibrium to suffer.' In other words, our bodies and minds react when we feel pressured to accomplish something or get something done and feel it's going to be very hard to do that… if it can be done. Stress occurs whether the situation is positive or negative. For instance, when you're going to have a party, you might feel stress as you get everything ready for company. The party is going to be fun, so this is a positive situation. Or you might feel stressed because you have four papers due on Friday for four different classes. That's negative stress! Regardless of the cause, stress is hard on your body and mind."

"How do you respond to stress?"

[Pause.]

"What are some healthy ways to respond to stress?"

[Pause.]

"What kinds of exercise do you do? Does it make you feel better?"

[Pause.]

A Closer Look at Diet and Exercise

Have four girls read the journal entries aloud. After each entry ask the class members to raise their hands if they can personally relate to that entry. Then ask if they know people like the journal writers. After all entries are read, have a more in-depth discussion.

Journal 1

Had fun at school today...skipped the noon salad and bought a bag of M&M's instead...ate them during class and Mr. Nose Whistles When He Talks didn't even see me. Stopped with my chicas at the mall after school for a grande vanilla latte with extra whip. Mom was taking a little longer with dinner, so I called my friends. They got irritated with me crunching on chips, so I switched to texting instead. Went to the game tonight and couldn't resist my favorites...Milk Duds and a Diet Coke. Finally got home at nine. I slipped a small pizza into the oven to go with my energy drink. I need to stay awake to get my studying done. What a day!

I wonder why my face won't clear up?

Journal 2

Got excused from gym today...told the teacher I was dizzy. I did feel kinda tired, but really, I just didn't want to jump those silly hurdles. Got a ride to the library after school...who wants to walk 8 blocks? Got home and read a really cool book I got from the library. Claire called and asked me to go skating with her youth group tonight, but I'm just not up for it. Besides, this mystery is really exciting. She said the skating will be fun, but the guys ask her to skate with them...and they never ask me. I'm happy to stay home and read.

Journal 3

Hmmm...where do I start? Well, in class today this girl was like, "I can't believe that you are so tiny! Do you ever eat?" I asked if she were joking. She said I was the skinniest girl she knows. I laughed. I guess this shirt is really flattering because I'm so not skinny. I eat all the time. At least that's what it feels like. This morning I ate 3 skittles for breakfast. I felt so bad about eating sugar for breakfast I only ate celery for lunch. I really would like to be skinny.

Journal 4

Woke up, felt great! I kicked back the covers and did a few crunches before stumbling to the shower. I read my Bible and prayed and then headed to school. What a day! I still can't believe it. They elected me basketball team captain. I never dreamed I'd be chosen! I was so excited I could hardly settle down at lunch, but I had my usual tuna salad. This afternoon we played our arch rivals. I managed to make four baskets! It was a fast game, but fun. Everyone gathered around me to talk afterward, and I missed the bus. I walked home and ate the apple I'd saved from lunch. Had just taken a bite when <u>Steve!!</u> yelled, "Hey, Claire!" My mouth was so full I couldn't answer. We both had a good laugh and talked all the way home. He asked me to homecoming!

"Now that we've read the journals, let me introduce the girls. Can you guess which journal entries each one wrote? Write down their names by their entries in your workbook.

- ❀ Inertia Isabelle
- ❀ Keeps Nibblin' Kaley
- ❀ Committed Claire
- ❀ No Energy Elise

"How many of you identified with Keeps Nibblin' Kaley? What was so familiar about her? Is her lifestyle healthy? Is yours? What changes could you make to be healthier?"

"How many of you identified with No Energy Elise? What was familiar? Is she healthy? Are you? Do you need to make changes?"

"How many of you identified with Inertia Isabelle? Why? Is her lifestyle healthy? Is yours? Are there changes to make?"

"How many of you identified with Committed Claire? What was so familiar? Is her lifestyle healthy? Is yours? What changes could you make to improve?"

The Truth About Calories

"We know that when we run, lift weights, play sports, and jog, we burn calories. But do you realize that every movement you make uses calories? Taking out the trash burns calories. Cleaning your room burns calories. Vacuuming burns calories. Walking home from school burns calories. We don't have to go to the school gym or track, use fancy exercise equipment, or play team sports to stay fit. Try doing a few sit-ups or squats the next time you settle down to watch your favorite TV show. Do some arm circles or lift some hand weights. Every sustained movement contributes to your good health."

"In your workbook write down some ways you can increase your movements daily."

"What kinds of activities did you come up with?"

It Adds Up

"Cheeseburgers, fries, and ice cream—we know these have many calories and a lot of fat that isn't good for us. We watch out for the big things, but often those little snacks here and there sneak under our radar. Just a handful of chips can be the same as ordering french fries.

"And liquid calories can really be sneaky. A small Frappuccino from Starbucks can have 340 calories and 14 grams of fat. Liquid calories add up quickly.

"We all enjoy treats now and then. The trick is knowing what to pick. With all the choices we have, it's sometimes easier to order the first thing we see, but that's not wise. The next time you get a craving for a Frappuccino, ask for nonfat milk or make it sugar free and sweeten it with a natural sugar substitute, such as Truvia (from the stevia plant). Need a cheeseburger fix? Try a junior cheeseburger and skip the mayo.

"Becoming conscious of every morsel we put into our mouths will make a huge difference in our consumption.

 "Let's be calorie detectives for a minute. I'll name some foods, and you guess how much exercise it takes to burn the calories, okay?

❀ How long would you have to walk to burn off two double-stuffed Oreos?

❀ How long would you have to dance to burn off a handful of chips?

❀ How long would you have to swim to burn off one candy bar?

❀ How long would you have to bike to burn off one slice of chocolate cake?

❀ How long would you have to jog to burn off one 12-ounce regular soda?

- 2 double stuffed Oreos = 1 hour of riding a bike
- 1 handful of chips = 20 minutes of water aerobics
- 1 candy bar = 35 minutes of swimming laps
- 1 slice of chocolate cake = 1 hour of ballroom dancing
- 1 12-ounce soda = 30 minutes of walking

"Isn't that amazing? I'm always surprised at how much exercise it takes to burn the calories from my favorite foods. Why not look up more information on exercise, calories, and specific foods on the web?"

Quick and Easy Exercises

"With all you have going on, it may be hard to think about adding one more thing. But getting involved in sports or regular physical activity will help you feel better and give you energy. Add more movement when you can. Here are a few ideas to try. Write them in your workbooks so you'll remember.

❀ walk, jog, or run every chance you get

❀ stretch to relax your body and ease tension

❀ swim for great all-around exercise

❀ get an exercise DVD and do what it says

❀ use weights or soup cans and do bicep curls

- ❀ do shoulder presses (pumping hands up and down above your head)

- ❀ leg squats (legs wide apart and lunging forward)

- ❀ crunches

"In your book are two exercises, how long to do them, and the specific muscles being targeted. These are great to start your day. Do them regularly. And you can find more exercise ideas at the library and online."

Review the exercises in class and do a few of them together. Consider reviewing the muscle groups in case the girls don't know what "glutes" and "quadriceps" are.

Move! Move! Move!

"In addition to muscle strengthening and stretching, there are exercises that strengthen your heart or cardiovascular system. These are aerobic exercises that get your heart pumping and blood moving. A good goal is to get at least 20 minutes of cardiovascular exercise in a day.

"Exercise helps us lose weight and feel better. It causes our bodies to release additional endorphins, growth hormones, and other beneficial chemicals. You'll also be more alert and sleep better. And all these benefits are free!"

Reflecting Christ

"Who can recite 1 Corinthians 6:19-20…or at least tell me what it's about?"

Do you not know that your body is a temple of the Holy Spirit, who is in you, whom you have received from God? You are not your own; you were bought at a price. Therefore honor God with your body.

"It's important that we take care of our bodies because the Holy Spirit resides within us. Even more important is keeping in shape spiritually.

Discussion "Here's a great idea! Why not get in shape physically and spiritually at the same time? For instance, 'walk with the Lord' daily. Spend time talking with God, singing praises, listening, and meditating on His Word. What other ways could you incorporate physical and spiritual exercise into your day?"

Run the Race of Faith

"We've talked about the need for training to run marathons. The same holds true for the Christian life. To develop stamina and strength, we need to study and know God's Word and principles. We want to know His guidelines and wisdom so we can accomplish His plans and be good representatives for Him.

"This takes discipline—self-discipline. Remember Hebrews 12:11? *'No discipline seems pleasant at the time, but painful, later on, however, it produces a harvest of righteousness and peace for those trained by it.'*"

Write from Your Heart

Discuss the questions in the student workbook in class or have your girls work on them at home. For the next class, ask each girl to bring a Bible, pencil, and casual and dress shoes.

3

Positively Poised
A Graceful Guide to Posture

Purpose

This charm lesson teaches good posture habits. The girls will also better understand the importance of their walk with Christ.

Prayer

Gracious God, help me walk the Christian path in such a way that I model You for these girls. Reveal Your wisdom to me and the girls so we will grow in You. In Jesus' name. Amen.

Ponder

"And we pray [for God to fill you with knowledge of His will] in order that you may live a life worthy of the Lord and may please him in every way: bearing fruit in every good work, growing in the knowledge of God" (Colossians 1:10).

Preparation

If someone in your organization has had modeling training or charm school instruction, ask her to be a guest speaker for this section. And don't underestimate your ability to teach posture and carriage. Study the illustrations and practice the various techniques. This is a fun lesson to learn and teach.

Throughout this instruction period, allow the girls time to practice each point as you describe it. Make helpful suggestions and corrections. As the various posture and carriage problems are discussed, choose two girls from the class to be demonstrators. Let one girl show the graceful body position or movement, while the other portrays the ungraceful pose. By observing the contrasting poses and movements side by side, the girls will discern the differences more quickly and become more aware of the unflattering effects of poor posture.

Equipment

- ❀ string
- ❀ strong adhesive tape
- ❀ a plumb bob or weight for a plumb line
- ❀ a full-length mirror

Position the mirror straight up and down. Tape a long piece of string at the top center of the mirror. Affix the plumb bob or weight to the string so it swings slightly above the floor. You now have a plumb line.

Personalize

- ❀ Choose two girls before class to role-play *Sloppy Sadie* and *Pretty Petunia*. Ask them to exaggerate their movements and attitudes.

    Sloppy Sadie slouches, sits with her legs spread out, and is rude and obnoxious.

    Pretty Petunia walks straight, sits with her knees together and her legs neatly crossed at the ankles. She is kind and considerate.

- ❀ Place two chairs at the front of the room facing the class.

Getting Started

"Hi, class! I'm so glad you came today. Let's get started with prayer."

Pray for God to open your minds and hearts to His wisdom. Praise Him for each girl that came to class.

"Today we're going to work on our second memory verse. Let's turn to the 'Connecting with Christ' section and read 2 Corinthians 5:17 together.

"If anyone is in Christ, he is a new creation, the old has gone, the new has come!"

"This week work on memorizing this verse, and you can recite it next week. Now, let me introduce you to two girls. Maybe you've even met them before."

Have the girls you asked to role-play go out and then enter in character. Have them sit in front of the class.

"Which one do you think is known as *Sloppy Sadie?* What did you notice about her?"

"What did you notice about *Pretty Petunia?*"

Ready for the Party?

"Let's say you're invited to a party. You're so excited that you go out and buy a beautiful new shirt with your babysitting money. The night of the party you try the shirt on with every pair of pants you own and finally settle on black jeans. You fix your hair and put on your makeup. Everything is perfect. Add the finishing touch of your favorite earrings, and you're ready to go. You're sure to turn heads when you walk in.

"But wait! What will people really notice?

"The finishing touch isn't your favorite earrings. The final step in your appearance is how you present yourself—your posture. Does that seem odd? Even the cutest girl with the most put-together outfit loses glamour when she walks into a room hunched over or with her head hanging down.

"Picture the walk and posture of a linebacker. Now picture the walk and posture of a beautiful runway model. Do you see the difference? The loveliness of the model is enhanced because she stands tall and straight and exudes confidence. The linebacker looks solid and tough as he strides down the hall with his shoulders square.

"Like your workbook says, one dictionary definition of 'poised' is 'a graceful, controlled way of standing, moving, or performing an action.' A dictionary definition of 'carriage' is 'manner of bearing the body: posture.' So essentially we're going to talk about posture and gracefulness."

Creating a Comfortable and Graceful Stance

"Let's start at the top and attack the problem 'head first.' How we carry our heads plays a large role in our overall appearance. For instance, think of how much beauty a vibrant rose loses when it droops.

"A sagging head triggers a downward chain reaction that ends with a slumpy, jellyroll look. Try it. Let your head sag and then record what happens in your workbook."

"What did you notice? I noticed…

- ✿ my shoulders slumped
- ✿ my chest caved in
- ✿ my waistline thickened

"And when our waistlines 'disappear,' our chests and hips look squashed together. Not only have we lost about one inch in body height, but we've also added about an inch around our middles.

"What can we do to improve our appearance? For perfect body balance, we need to line up our heads with our bodies."

"Girls, put your books down and let's all stand up. We're going to practice holding our heads up and standing confidently.

"1. Keep your head up:

❀ pull your head up—but not with your chin. Pull your head up and back from behind using your neck muscles

❀ stretch the top of your head upward until you feel a tugging behind your ears

❀ at the same time push gently downward with your shoulders

❀ keep as much distance as possible between your head and shoulders

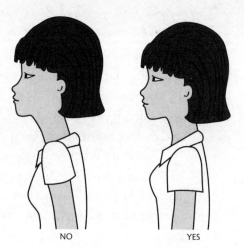

NO   YES

"2. Keep your head squarely on our shoulders:

❀ never hang your head forward over your chest

❀ deliberately pull back with your neck muscles until the center of your ear is lined up vertically with the center of your shoulder

❀ ask a friend to check your head position by holding a pencil vertically at your ear lobe. Does it line up with the center of your shoulder? Pull your head backward until it does

"3. Keep your shoulders straight:

❀ avoid letting your shoulders go forward over your chest

❀ avoid pushing your shoulders back like a soldier standing at attention. Instead, a small amount of downward pressure on your shoulders will keep them low and relaxed

"4. Let your arms hang naturally:

❀ don't stiffen your arms or clench your fists

❀ keep your elbows bent slightly

❀ your thumbs should be resting at your side

"5. Keep your chest from sagging:

❀ don't puff your chest up and out like a balloon

❀ hold your chest high enough to create plenty of space between your hips and your ribs. This silhouette creates a more flattering figure

"6. Keep your knees relaxed:

❀ avoid locking your knees. If you lock your knees, you'll notice that your back and hips are uncomfortable and swayed. Your weight is thrown forward and your tummy pushes out

"7. Point your feet forward and keep them together:

❀ divide your weight evenly between both legs

YES

❀ stand comfortably and naturally

❀ don't put all or most of your weight on your toes or the back of your feet."

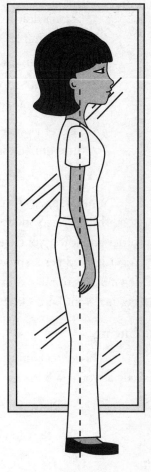

Check your girls' postures using the mirror and plumb line you set up before class. Direct each girl to take turns standing sideways in front of the mirror so the plumb line is centered on the lobe of the ear. If their posture is in correct balance, the plumb line will bisect the body at the lobe of the ear, at the center of the shoulder bone, at the center of the hips, and will come to about an inch in front of the ankle bone. The plumb line doesn't lie. If the body is off balance, help the young lady realign herself. Let her get the feel of what it's like to be in proper alignment.

Walking and Sitting

"Now that we've practiced standing, let's see what sitting and walking gracefully entail. Let's all stand up.

"First, check your posture. 'The loveliest roses have the longest stems.' Stretch and pull yourself 'up,' but remain comfortable."

Walking

"Now step forward, placing your heel down first, softly and lightly. A gentle push ahead from the other foot will roll you forward smoothly. Don't plop your heels down or force them down with jarring thuds. Walk in a straight line, imagining you're following a chalk line.

❀ Your feet should be pointing straight ahead.

❀ Glide smoothly.

❀ Don't bounce up and down like a rubber ball.

❀ Remain straight from the hips up.

❀ Are your head and chest slanting forward, getting ahead of the rest of you?

❀ Are you leading with your head or "pointing with your nose"?

❀ Is your head in line over your hips?

❀ Lead with your knees and thighs.

❀ Swing out smoothly from your hips.

"What are some things to watch for?

❀ Don't touch your knees together. They should *almost* brush.

❀ Don't overreach with your stride; keep it moderate.

NO   NO   YES

- ❀ Don't drag or click your heels; don't shuffle.

- ❀ Don't over-swing your arms. Keep your shoulders relaxed and arm movements minimal.

- ❀ Don't wobble or sway your hips unnecessarily.

- ❀ Don't wear shoes that hurt.

"What happens if you drop something? Place one foot in front of the other and lower yourself with both knees together and bent, spine straight, and head erect. Reach down and pick up the item, then use your leg muscles to raise your body again, keeping your spine and head straight. Don't just bend over because your buttocks will be prominently outlined behind you, which isn't the best look."

Sitting

To help break up the instructions, you can demonstrate or have various girls demonstrate each one as you share it.

"Okay, now let's try sitting.

- ❀ Slowly back up to your chair until you feel the front edge with both legs.

- ❀ Place one foot a bit under the chair to provide good balance.

- ❀ Bend your knees and slowly move down until sitting, keeping back straight.

- ❀ Keep your hips tucked under you.

- ❀ Sit on the edge of the chair.

- ❀ Slide back gracefully in one movement, easing yourself into place.

"Good job!

"If you're wearing a dress or skirt, as you lower yourself into a chair run the back of your thumbs down the sides of your skirt to keep it wrinkle free.

"And once you're sitting down, remain graceful. Sit tall with your knees together, ankles together, one foot slightly ahead of the other, hands resting lightly in your lap.

"When crossing your legs, cross them well above the knee and keep your legs close together. Press the hanging foot close to the ankle of the other foot. Point your toes

YES

downward. Another option is to have your knees together and cross your ankles, drawing your legs slightly to one side.

"Keep your feet planted naturally in front of you. Avoid twisting and turning them around your chair and pushing them under the chair.

"Your legs should always be in front of the chair.

"Take your seat in a calm, graceful manner. Avoid sprawling like a rag doll. Find a comfortable, upright position as quickly and quietly as possible. Avoid shifting back and forth so you don't disrupt others. Avoid reclining in your chair.

NO

"Keep your arms down and relaxed. Don't fold them because you may look bored or uninterested. Place your hands gracefully in your lap. Avoid fidgeting and fussing with your face or body."

Going Up and Down Stairs
(This isn't in the student workbook.)

"To go up and down stairs gracefully, maintain the same posture as when standing. Keep your head and chin level. Don't stare down at the steps or lean forward. Look up and ahead."

Entering a Room (This isn't in the student workbook.)

"Now that you can stand with perfect poise, how do you enter a room maintaining your gracefulness? Glide smoothly and effortlessly. Keep your head up and be alert. Smile. Be friendly and enjoy yourself. Keep your conversation pleasant."

 *Reflecting Christ*

 Discussion
"What is the difference between a girl who walks in confidence and one who walks in confidence in herself only?

"Will someone look up and read Philippians 4:13 for us?"

I can do everything through him [Jesus] who gives me strength.

"How does this relate to being confident? Share some examples of times when you thought you couldn't continue, but God gave you the strength and wisdom to move forward."

"Your workbook mentions how toddlers learn to walk. First they crawl, then they stand, next they take a few wobbly steps, and then they're really walking. They fall, get back up, and try again. Our spiritual walks are much like that. We try, we fall, we get back up, we try again. What have you decided to do…but failed…but picked yourself up and kept at it until you were successful…or are still working toward being successful?"

You might want to give examples from your life too.

"What do you think the question 'Does your walk match your talk' means? Joshua 24:15 says, *'Choose for yourselves this day whom you will serve…but as for me and my household, we will serve the* LORD.' Who are you serving? If you're serving Christ, how are you doing it?

"Let's take a look at one of our Connect with Christ verses. Will someone look up and read Philippians 4:8?"

> *Finally, brothers, whatever is true, whatever is noble, whatever is right, whatever is pure, whatever is lovely, whatever is admirable—if anything is excellent or praiseworthy—think about such things.*

"How can we develop 'Christlike character' as we walk with Christ? Colossians 3:12-14 tells us. Who will look that up for us?"

> *As God's chosen people, holy and dearly loved, clothe yourselves with compassion, kindness, humility, gentleness and patience. Bear with each other and forgive whatever grievances you may have against one another. Forgive as the Lord forgave you. And over all these virtues put on love, which binds them all together in perfect unity.*

"That's quite an assignment, isn't it? As your workbook reminds you, we don't have to be intimidated. The Lord will give us the strength and courage we need to follow Him. And we have the Holy Spirit living inside us to encourage us and remind us of Jesus' love and teachings. Each day we'll learn more about how to walk in His love…uprightly…honestly…humbly. This walk produces a joyful, happy spring in our steps!"

Write from Your Heart

If you choose, discuss the questions in the student workbook under "Write from Your Heart." Or remind the girls to answer them at home and then briefly talk about them at the next meeting.

"For the next class, bring a headband or scrunchy; a towel; cotton balls or squares; a small, stand-up makeup mirror; and some makeup samples if you have them.

"Now, let's close our time with a prayer adapted from Psalm 19:14:

> *"Dear heavenly Father, may the words of our mouths and the meditations of our hearts be pleasing in Your sight, O Lord, our Rock and our Redeemer. In Jesus' name we pray. Amen."*

4

Let's Face It
Your Radiant Countenance

Purpose

Developing a beautiful countenance, which radiates from a heart being changed daily by Christ. We'll also learn the practical steps of how to care for our faces through proper cleaning and makeup.

Prayer

Dear God, just as You brought light out of darkness, help me guide these girls to see their natural beauty. Show them how to let their inner light shine for You. For Your glory and in the name of Christ I pray. Amen.

Ponder

"For God, who said, 'Let light shine out of darkness,' made his light shine in our hearts to give us the light of the knowledge of the glory of God in the face of Christ" (2 Corinthians 4:6).

Preparation

❀ If you know a cosmetic specialist, consider having her come to the class to demonstrate keeping faces healthy and applying makeup (if desired).

❀ Set up area to wash faces and practice putting on makeup (if desired). You'll need water, small bowls, and facial cleanser in small cups or on wax paper. Have extra supplies handy in case some girls need them.

✿ Last week you asked each girl to bring a headband or scrunchy; a towel; cotton balls or squares; a small, stand-up makeup mirror; and makeup samples. Bring enough supplies in case the girls forgot or don't have these materials.

Equipment

- extra headbands and scrunchies
- extra towels
- facial cleanser (1 tsp. per girl in small cups or on wax paper)
- cotton balls or squares
- extra stand-up makeup mirrors
- makeup samples
- bowls or basins for holding water
- warm water
- towels or paper towels to clean up spilled water

Makeup supplies to show and explain to girls

- foundation (cream and powder)
- translucent powder (optional)
- blush or bronzer
- mascara
- lip gloss
- makeup sponges
- eyebrow pencil
- tweezers (optional)
- eyelash curler (optional)

✿ Ask two girls ahead of time to act out these characters as you describe them. Have them exaggerate the girls' actions.

Grumpy Gertrude tromps into the room. She's complaining about everything. She alternates between having her head down and staring at everybody. Her clothes are unmatched and askew.

Sunshine Savannah strolls into the room with a bright smile and a wave for everyone. She is optimistic, and always sees the good in everyone. She tries to say something positive to everyone she meets. Her clothes match and are neat.

Getting Started

"Hi, girls! I'm so glad you're here. Let's ask God to bless our time together."

Pray for God to open your minds and hearts to His wisdom. Praise Him for each girl who came to class.

"Let's review our second memory verse, 2 Corinthians 5:17. Who wants to recite it by memory for us?"

If anyone is in Christ, he is a new creation, the old has gone, the new has come!

Discussion

"I'd like to introduce you to two girls. The first is *Grumpy Gertrude.*
"Notice how she tromps into the room, complaining about everything. First she looks down, and then she stares at everybody. Her clothes are unmatched and askew.
"Now here comes *Sunshine Savannah.* See how she strolls into the room with a bright smile and a wave for everyone? She's optimistic, always seeing the good in everyone. She says something positive to everyone she meets. Her clothes match and she looks very neat."

Discuss the differences between the two girls. Point out what's good and what's not so good.

Saving Face

"Every girl wants to be pretty, but not every girl is born a classic beauty. Noses are too long, chins too pointed, eyes too close, mouths too generous, lips too thin. All of us have features we wish looked different. Add to these imperfections pimples, acne, braces, and/or eyeglasses, and we can throw ourselves across our beds and sob, 'I'm hopeless! I was never meant to be attractive.'

"It's time to stop crying over what we *wish* was different and embrace who God made us to be. God is the author of beauty! As His daughters, He wants us to have a special appeal so that others will notice us, want what we have, and then come to know and admire Him.

"Are you thinking, *If God wanted me to be pretty, why didn't He give me perfect features?* The answer is simple. You can be attractive and appealing with the features you have. Furthermore, perfect features are often uninteresting and uninspiring. Think how boring the world would be if everyone walked around perfect all the time. So let's embrace the features He's given us and radiate the beauty of Christ! The joy that sparkles from your eyes and your warm, friendly smile create and reflect true charm."

Changing Our Thoughts

"Your workbook quotes 2 Corinthians 10:5: '*We take captive every thought to make it obedient to Christ,*' to emphasize that who we are inside is what makes our outsides radiate peace and joy. Admittedly, getting a handle on our thoughts can be tough.

"The first thing we need to know is what to change our critical thoughts to. Let's read Philippians 4:8."

Ask a student to look it up and read it out loud.

> *Finally, brothers, whatever is true, whatever is noble, whatever is right, whatever is pure, whatever is lovely, whatever is admirable—if anything is excellent or praiseworthy—think about such things.*

"What a great verse! When we realize we're comparing ourselves to others or wishing we looked different, we need to mentally say, 'Stop! This isn't what God wants me to do.' Then we can recite Philippians 4:8 (that's why we're going to memorize it!) and do what it says.

"This takes practice, but keep at it. You'll see a difference in how you view yourself…and those around you will sense your confidence and joy in the Lord.

"God created us how we are. Who will look up Psalm 139 for us? [Choose someone.] Great. Please read verses 13 through 16."

> *You created my inmost being; you knit me together in my mother's womb. I praise you because I am fearfully and wonderfully made; your works are wonderful, I know that full well. My frame was not hidden from you when I was made in the secret place. When I was woven together in the depths of the earth, your eyes saw my unformed body. All the days ordained for me were written in your book before one of them came to be.*

"God also knows everything we'll encounter in this life that will affect what our bodies look like. So let's not put down what God created! One of our God-given jobs is to be good stewards of what He's given us, and that includes our bodies.

"Today we're going to discover how to take care of our faces so our skin will be healthy, and we'll feel good about how we're taking care of ourselves."

Keeping Our Faces Healthy

"The two essentials to facial beauty are to…

✿ renew our minds with verses such as Philippians 4:8

✿ refuse to play the comparison game

"Now let's go over the day-to-day care we can give our faces."

Washing Our Faces

"Cleaning our faces seems basic, doesn't it? But there are some tips that will help you keep your face healthier. In front of you should be some water, a little bit of facial cleanser, a mirror, and a towel. Let's get started!

✿ Lightly dampen your face with water.

✿ Dip your finger or a corner of the towel into the cleanser (or use the applicator if provided) and gently dab cleanser onto your face.

✿ Massage cleanser around in outward-upward motions. This gently pushes the skin up instead of pulling it down, which helps prevent wrinkles.

✿ Wash your entire face, especially the nose area where dirt tends to get trapped.

✿ Rinse thoroughly with warm water, making sure to get rid of all the residue from the soap and any makeup you may have been wearing.

✿ Pat your face dry with a towel. *Don't rub your face* because this may irritate your skin."

More Tips for Facial Health (This is in the student workbook.)

✿ Wash your face when you get up and before you go to bed.

✿ Depending on your age and skin type, follow the cleanser with toner. You can ask your mom or a cosmetologist about whether your skin needs it. Toner closes up pores after cleaning, so it's important to use if you have oily skin.

✿ Always use sunscreen when you're outside.

✿ Moisturize your skin often.

✿ Drink lots of water. When your body is hydrated, so is your skin. Water also cleanses impurities out of your body, which promotes healthy skin.

✿ Watch your diet. Good nutrition keeps your skin healthy.

Skin Blemishes (This is in the student workbook.)

"No matter how conscientious you are about keeping your skin clean, there will be times when you'll get pimples or break out. That's part of teen life…and almost everyone has experienced it at one time or another. Don't let this ruin your social life. Having a few blemishes isn't a good reason to stay home. People still want to see you! For special events, apply concealer (special makeup) to downplay the problem.

"If skin eruptions persist, talk with your parents. Ask them if you need to consult a dermatologist. He or she may prescribe medicine to help clear up your skin and counter what is causing the problem. Severe irritations and acne can cause scarring, so take good care of your skin."

Makeup

"I'm sure you've noticed there are many different looks when it comes to applying makeup. The best idea is to strive for naturalness. We want to *enhance* our features, not create them. By skillfully applying makeup, people will notice our natural beauty and not the fact that we're wearing makeup.

"Here are some basic makeup supplies that people use. Everything is optional. Use what you feel comfortable with."

Supplies

✿ foundation (cream or powder)

✿ translucent powder (optional)

✿ blush or bronzer

✿ mascara

✿ lip gloss, lip balm

✿ makeup sponges

✿ eyebrow pencil

✿ tweezers (optional)

✿ eyelash curler (optional)

Choose two girls to serve as models. Explain and demonstrate how to apply foundation, lipstick, blush, and so on. The goal is a natural look so she doesn't look like she's wearing makeup…or at least not a lot of makeup. (If you've invited a cosmetician, she can do the demonstration while you explain…or she can do both. Let the cosmetician know ahead of time that you want to emphasize a natural look.)

For the second model, apply quite a bit of cheek color, eyebrow pencil, eye shadow, and so on, to show the negative effects of too much makeup. (Don't go overboard though…keep your demonstration realistic.)

This visual presentation will make a greater impact than verbally telling the girls not to use too much makeup.

Note: The following information is identical to the student workbook.

Foundation

"Foundation is the most important part of makeup. Here are a few practical pointers.

✿ Determine your skin type: normal, oily, dry, or 'combination skin' (your mom or a cosmetician can help).

✿ Evaluate the *texture* of your skin.

✿ Notice your skin *tone* (color). Is your skin light, medium, or dark?

"When you go to the store, these areas will be covered in the product descriptions. It's a good idea to ask someone who knows about makeup to go with you and help you. You want to purchase the appropriate foundation for your skin. You also want the color to blend in with your natural color so you don't have a 'foundation line' between your face and neck.

"To apply foundation, follow these general guidelines.

✿ Wash your face. For the last rinse, use cold water to help close your pores and keep makeup on top of your skin.

✿ You can add moisturizer or lotion if you'd like. If you'll be outside, use moisturizer that includes sunscreen of SPF-15 or higher.

✿ Apply six or so dabs of foundation in various spots on your face (a little goes a long way).

✿ Use a makeup sponge to gently spread the foundation, blending it with your skin so there are no visible lines.

✿ Apply a light coating of translucent powder to set the foundation (optional)."

Concealer

"Concealer is special makeup that covers blemishes (including dark circles under eyes and skin discolorations). It comes in a solid stick, liquid, cream, and medicated. There are specialized concealers for acne, dark circles, allergy sufferers, and those who want waterproof makeup.

✿ Choose light, medium, or dark, depending on your skin and foundation color. Girls, be careful not to go too dark. And foundation doesn't work well as a tan substitute. It won't look real, and there will be lines where the foundation ends and your natural skin begins.

❀ Dab it on and lightly cover blemish. If you rub it in too much, it won't conceal the problem area.

❀ A little goes a long way."

Powder

"Powder 'sets' your foundation and prevents smearing or caking. Some makeup brands don't need powder, so check the labeling and directions. Getting advice from your mom or a cosmetologist is a great idea too.

❀ Use the powder puff and lightly pat on your face.

❀ Be gentle, and don't rub it in."

Blush and Bronzer

"There are many choices and colors available, so experiment until you find a few colors you like.

❀ Dab onto cheeks or over cheekbones (a little goes a long way).

❀ Carefully smooth and blend in an up and outward motion with a makeup sponge."

Eye Makeup

"Eye shadow can highlight your eyes and bring a light shimmer to your look.

❀ Apply lightly.

❀ Close your eye and brush on shadow from below your eyebrow to your lashes.

❀ To add depth, in the 'crease' only, use a darker color.

"Too much eye shadow will detract from your overall look, so use it sparingly.

"You can lengthen your eyelashes with mascara.

❀ Brush on, moving from your eyelid out.

❀ If too much is put on, it cakes and flakes.

"If you are using bright eye shadow, go easy on the lip gloss…and vice versa. Drawing attention to only one area at a time emphasizes cohesiveness and calm."

Lip Gloss, Lip Balm, Lipstick

❀ Lip gloss provides moisturizer, a shine, and often some soft color. Light shading can enhance the natural color in your lips. Light coloring can also pick up some of the color in your cheeks to give you a natural-looking glow. Lip gloss is perfect for casual occasions.

❀ Lip balm provides moisturizer and is usually clear.

❀ Lipstick usually includes moisturizer and provides color from soft to glaring. I suggest you stay light on the color, girls.

"Apply lip balm, lip gloss, or lipstick directly from the tube. Place a tissue between your lips and gently press your lips together to 'blot' or remove any excess lipstick. Make sure to remove any lipstick from the inside portion of your lips to avoid getting lipstick on your teeth. Another way to keep your teeth clean is to make an 'O' with your lips, stick your finger in your mouth, and quickly pull it out (the disadvantage with this is that you have to wash your hands afterward.)

For a more formal way of applying lipstick, follow these steps:

✿ moisturize your lips

✿ outline your lips with lip liner

✿ use a clean lip brush and rub over lipstick

✿ rub brush gently over your lips

✿ place a tissue between your lips and gently press your lips together to blot

✿ touch up as needed"

Special Considerations (This is not in the student workbook.)

"If you have braces, wear glasses, or have prominent skin features such as freckles, the best thing to do is make them part of who you are (because they are!). These things do not detract from your overall look unless you're self-conscious about them. So accept how you were created and whatever help you need to see and make them part of your fashion statement."

What Your Face Says (Student workbook doesn't have all this information.)

"Have you given much thought to what your facial expressions tell people? If we could see our own faces all day, we'd probably be surprised at how often we aren't smiling or putting forth a positive look. If we frown a lot, clench our teeth, or narrow our eyes, our face muscles settle into patterns and people see negativity or apathy or uncertainty.

"Let's take a few minutes and assume some facial expressions we unknowingly show others. As you look into your mirrors, I'll ask you a few questions and help you evaluate your general look.

✿ Is your brow relaxed and smooth?

✿ Are your lips in a smile or are the corners tipping up slightly?

✿ Are your eyes open and relaxed?

✿ Is your chin at a relaxed angle (not jutting out or being tucked into your neck)?

"Be conscious of your facial expressions. Let a happy glow linger. And above all, be generous with smiles. Smiles make you and the people around you happier.

"Some people have acquired some habits that aren't very flattering. Here are some to avoid:

✿ biting or chewing your lips

✿ moistening your lips frequently

✿ waving your tongue over your lips

✿ gritting your teeth

✿ clenching your jaw

✿ jerking your jaw from side to side

✿ pursing your lips"

"Why not keep mirrors near where you study and talk on the phone so you can check your facial expressions? You girls can help each other by pointing out any of these habits in expressions…but only if you're asked to. Becoming conscious of your mannerisms is the first step toward handling them."

Reflecting Christ

"We've been discovering how to make our faces healthier and more attractive through proper care, makeup, and facial posture. But there's another vital source for ultimate beauty. Have you heard that God runs a 'beauty shop'? His love will make your face glow and shine! This look is something we can't create ourselves. God adds this crowning beauty treatment. If we let Him, He begins deep within our hearts and transforms us so that every day we experience and reflect more of His love and care. This makes our faces glow and exude love to those around us."

Write from Your Heart

If you'd like, you can go through the "Write from Your Heart" questions with your girls or have them answer them at home and briefly go over them at the next meeting.

"Girls, at our next meeting we're going to talk about hands and manicures. Won't that be fun! Here are some items you'll want to bring. Write them down so you won't forget!

✿ two small bowls big enough to soak your fingers in

✿ a nail file

✿ nail brushes

✿ cotton balls or squares

✿ a cuticle stick

✿ basecoat fingernail polish

✿ fingernail polish

✿ top-coat fingernail polish

"See you at our next meeting."

5

Hands to Serve; Feet to Move
Beautiful Hands and Healthy Feet

Purpose

To learn how to care for our hands, and to use our hands in ways that honor the Lord and serve others.

Prayer

Heavenly Father, help me model and explain servanthood to these precious girls. Be with me as I draw on the Proverbs 31 woman to explain service. I want to "turn on" their enthusiasm to use their hands and feet for You. Amen.

Ponder

"She opens her arms to the poor and extends her hands to the needy" (Proverbs 31:20).

Preparation

- ❀ paper towels
- ❀ buckets with warm, sudsy water to fill 2 bowls per girl
- ❀ polish remover
- ❀ cotton balls
- ❀ nail brushes
- ❀ orange stick/cuticle stick

- ✿ nail buffer
- ✿ lotion
- ✿ soap or perfume oil to put in finger water
- ✿ nail file
- ✿ basecoat fingernail polish
- ✿ fingernail polish
- ✿ top-coat fingernail polish

You've asked girls to bring these, but bring extras in case some forget.

- ✿ bowls for soaking fingers
- ✿ nail files
- ✿ nail brushes
- ✿ cotton balls or squares
- ✿ orange sticks/cuticle sticks
- ✿ basecoat fingernail polish
- ✿ fingernail polish
- ✿ top-coat fingernail polish
- ✿ Contact two girls in your class and ask them if they'll role-play the two "girls" you'll be introducing.

> *Yucky Hands Yoda* needs to have dirty hands, dirt under her fingernails, fingernails that are tattered and torn (use fake nails), and hands that *look* rough.

> *Manicured Molly* needs to have clean hands and fingernails that are filed and trimmed. She needs lotion she can be applying to her hands as she walks in.

Getting Started

"Hi, girls! I've really been looking forward to today's class. Our hands are so important to serving God and others. But before we get started, let's pray."

Lead the girls in prayer, asking God to open their hearts and minds to His wisdom and to help them discover how to look their best.

"Now let's read through our third core memory verse for this course. Turn to the 'Connecting with Christ' section and let's all read Colossians 3:24 out loud:

> " 'Whatever you do, work at it with all your heart, as working for the Lord, not for men, since you know that you will receive an inheritance from the Lord as a reward. It is the Lord Christ you are serving.'

"Isn't that a great verse? Work on memorizing it, and next week we'll recite it in class."

"Girls, there are two new girls I'd like you to meet: *Manicured Molly* and *Yucky Hands Yoda*. Here's Yoda."

Have Yucky Hands Yoda walk in.

"What do you notice about her hands?"

If necessary point out her dirty hands, the dirt under her fingernails, how tattered and torn the fingernails are, and that her hands appear rough.

"Here's Manicured Molly, the second girl I want you to meet."

Have Manicured Molly walk in.

"What do you notice about her hands?"

If necessary point out her clean hands, neat fingernails, the fact she's applying lotion to keep her skin hydrated.

You Can't Hide Your Hands

"Because most of us tend to use our hands when we talk, people notice them right away. We may be able to keep some secrets up our sleeves, but we can't hide our hands! Even if we try to keep them in our pockets, sit on them, hold them behind our backs, or keep them hidden, when we're not paying attention we'll soon be gesturing with them. We can't hide our hands for long.

"Look at your hands right now. Are they soft and clean? Or are they a bit dirty and rough? Are your fingernails smooth and shapely? Or are your nails jagged? Do you have nail polish on? Is it in good shape or peeling off?

"Our hands are wonderful tools we use all the time. When they aren't in good shape we may feel self-conscious. We shrink into the background, not letting our love for others shine. Thankfully, our hands can look great with a little care.

"Taking care of our hands goes beyond just looking good. Our hands encounter millions of germs. Everything we touch and every person we encounter carries germs. By washing our hands, we fight off diseases and illnesses."

Washing Our Hands

"How many of you have eaten without washing your hands? Have you ever not washed your hands after using the bathroom? And how often do you touch another person on the shoulder or arm or hand and not wash afterward? I won't ask for a show of hands, because at one time or another we've all been guilty of not washing our hands or not doing a thorough job at washing our hands. We get in a rush or don't want to take the time, so we do a halfhearted wash job.

"And, girls, sticking your hands under the water for two seconds doesn't count as washing. Let's go over the fundamentals:

❀ always use soap because it cleans and kills germs

❀ use hot or warm water to rinse off soap residue (water hot enough to kill germs would burn our hands so soap is crucial)

- ✿ lather soap well

- ✿ get under your fingernails (germs hide under nails)

- ✿ wash for a minimum of 20 seconds (sing "Happy Birthday" twice)

- ✿ be thorough

- ✿ pat or air dry to retain moisture

 Discussion   "When is it important to wash your hands?"

Make sure these areas are covered. Feel free to add more.

- ✿ before eating

- ✿ after eating

- ✿ after using the restroom

- ✿ after blowing your nose or coughing

- ✿ after changing diapers

- ✿ after playing with or petting animals

- ✿ after taking out the trash

- ✿ after cleaning your room

- ✿ after doing chores

"Washing our hands frequently is a good idea. Beautiful hands are clean, soft, and smooth. Use hand lotion often, especially after washing your hands or taking a shower. Applying it when your skin is wet helps lock in moisture.

"If you're going to be working with your hands in the yard, picking up trash for a community project, or using carpenter tools, wear work gloves to protect your skin. When you go outside in weather that is cold, windy, or stormy, pull on gloves or mittens. For messy or challenging chores around the house, slip on household gloves. Keep your hands nice by protecting them."

Fingernails and Manicures

"The appearance of your nails plays a big role in the loveliness of your hands. Fingernails are the focal point of your hand; the eye is naturally drawn to them. Having a balanced diet filled with fruits, vegetables, lean meats, and whole grains is one of the best ways to have beautiful nails.

"What are some specific foods you'll want to eat for good nail health? Write these down in your workbook! Foods such as eggs, oatmeal, nuts, apples, cucumbers, asparagus, onions, and grapes have been linked with nail strength and shine. Biotin-rich foods, such as soy, whole grains, and liver, are said to be very good for nail health. Make sure your diet includes essential fatty acids such as those found in salmon, nuts, seeds, and tuna, to keep your nails shiny and pliable. Unhealthy eating habits, from junk food to bulimia or anorexia, contribute to brittle nails, dry skin, and skin that peels easily.

"With regular care, you can keep your nails in lovely condition. You can pick up an inexpensive manicure set at most stores or create your own. You also might want to pick up some polish supplies. I suggest you write down the following items for your next shopping trip:

- ✿ nail file

- ✿ fingernail clippers

- ✿ nail brushes

- ✿ orange stick/cuticle stick

- ✿ nail buffer

- ✿ cotton balls or squares

- ✿ hand lotion

- ✿ fingernail polish remover

- ✿ basecoat fingernail polish

- ✿ fingernail polish

- ✿ top-coat fingernail polish

"Now, let's do some manicures. There are two bowls with *warm* water for each you. A few drops of soap (or perfumed oil) were added for a nice smell.

- ✿ Wash your hands.

- ✿ Pat your hands dry.

- ✿ Use a cuticle stick (an orange stick) to push your cuticles back. (Popsicle sticks or something with rounded edges can also be used.) Be careful. You don't want to tear or harm your cuticles. You're simply pushing them down so you can better apply nail polish. Don't add lotion or oil just before applying nail polish. (For cuticle maintenance, keep them moisturized to avoid hangnails. Keep moisturizers around the house, and whenever you come across one, use it. Carry lotion in your purse and backpack, and keep some in your school locker.)

- ✿ Lightly shape your nails with a nail file. Start at one side and file toward the center and over, creating a soft curve or gentle square shape. Don't file too deeply where your nails touch your skin. Move the file in one direction (don't go back and forth) to keep your nails strong and smooth. Shape all 10 nails similarly and to the same length for a uniform look.

- ✿ Buff nails.

Fingernail Polish

- ✿ Gently shake nail polish bottle.

- ✿ Apply basecoat nail polish over the entire nail, in sweeping, long strokes.

❀ Dip the brush in the bottle before each stroke.

❀ Remove excess polish from brush against the side of the bottle.

❀ Let basecoat dry (approx. 5 minutes).

❀ Apply second coat if desired and let dry.

❀ Put a top-coat of clear polish to seal and let dry.

❀ Add a drop of nail oil on each cuticle and gently rub in.

❀ Massage your hands and fingers with moisturizing lotion.

"Store nail polish bottles in a cool place.

"Polish looks pretty when it's kept up. Be sure to remove the polish or repair it at the first sign of chipping."

Lovely Hands Are Poised

"Are your hands constantly moving? Do you pick at your fingernails or cuticles a lot? Do you bite your nails? These are nervous habits that give the impression of restless anxiety. What are some other not-so-good habits that involve your hands?

❀ picking at your polish

❀ biting your nails

❀ cracking your knuckles

❀ playing with your rings or bracelet

❀ drumming on the table or chairs"

Discussion "As gracious young women, we want to portray quiet serenity and control. One way to break bad habits is to think of a substitute activity that isn't so noticeable. For instance, we could carry a small, soft ball to squeeze or a tiny, smooth, beautiful rock to rub. What else can we do to help us relax?"

Other activities might include praying, reciting Scripture, finding something to praise God about, counting or spelling words silently, and moving just one toe.

Discussion "As Christians, we have a bigger reason for keeping our hands well-groomed and clean. We are representatives for Christ and ambassadors for our heavenly King! What we do with our hands is important to God. He wants us to use our hands for His honor and glory. What are some ways we can use our hands to glorify God this week?"

A Quick Word About Feet

[The LORD]
set my feet on a rock
and gave me a first place to stand.
Psalm 40:2

"We've learned how to take care of our hands, but what about our feet? Feet don't usually get a lot of respect. Most people don't think their feet are very pretty, but when our feet hurt, our whole body hurts! Feet are important!"

Sole Care

"What may seem obvious, but something women are notorious for not doing, is wearing shoes that are the right size and comfortable. Let's engage our brains and do right by our feet.

❀ The next time you purchase shoes, have a salesperson take your foot measurements to make sure you know the length and width of your feet. Do this during the next few years too because you are growing.

❀ What you wear now will lead to how your feet feel and work in the coming years. Arch and ankle support are important. For instance, flip-flops are popular but provide no arch support. I'm not saying you can't wear summer shoes, but pay attention to how your feet feel, and act accordingly.

❀ Love your feet by occasionally soaking them in a tub of warm water. You may want to put in a few drops of lavender oil or half a cup of Epsom salts. Your feet will love you for it!

❀ After soaking, trim your toenails—straight across. You don't want to curve the nails because you might develop ingrown toenails, which can hurt and cause problems.

❀ Clean your toenails too.

❀ To prevent foot odor, wear natural fiber socks and change them often. Keep your shoes clean and sprinkle a little baking soda inside. Another idea is to put a fabric softener sheet in them at night to absorb any smells. (Don't forget to take them out before you put your shoes on.) If odor is a big problem, talk to your parents about getting some over-the-counter medicines that help with this problem.

❀ Athlete's foot isn't just for athletes. You can get this fungus from the gym floor or any public place where you go barefoot. If your feet are itching and you see red patches, especially by or between your toes, you may have athlete's foot. Talk to your parents or your teacher. You can buy inexpensive athlete's foot treatments in the foot section of pharmacies or drug stores. Athlete's foot will not go away on its own, so you need to take action.

- There are many "smell good" lotions and creams for feet available. Rub them in and let your feet dry. Your feet will feel great!

- Girls, I'm sorry, but high heels are *not* good for your feet. They raise havoc with your feet and back. Go for a lower heel if you feel compelled to wear heels.

- Put on clean socks every day.

- Do pedicures with your mom and/or friend. It feels good and makes your feet look pretty. Massage lotion into each other's feet as an added bonus for both of you.

"One very moving experience is to wash someone's feet. This is a beautiful way to show love and heart for service. Jesus did it as a model for us:

"'Jesus knew that the Father had put all things under his power, and that he had come from God and was returning to God; so he got up from the meal, took off his outer clothing, and wrapped a towel around his waist. After that, he poured water into a basin and began to wash his disciples' feet, drying them with the towel that was wrapped around him' (John 13:3-5).

"Let us do likewise."

 *Reflecting Christ*

*She opens her arms to the poor and
extends her hands to the needy.*

Proverbs 31:20

Share Proverbs 31:20 and then brainstorm with your girls on ideas for how they can serve their families, their communities, and people in their churches. Have them list 10 ideas in their workbooks. Ask them to commit to doing at least one of the suggestions this week. If desired, you can encourage them to do some of the activities together.

Write from Your Heart

If you'd like, you can go over the questions in the student workbook or have them answer them at home and briefly discuss them at the next meeting.

In the student workbook the girls are asked to memorize Proverbs 31:13 or 31:20. Let them know they'll be reciting their choice at the next meeting.

"Girls, for our next class, bring hairbrushes and stand-up makeup mirrors."

6

The "Mane" Attraction
Hair That Won't Steal the Show

Purpose

To help girls see the joy in caring for their hair and finding the right style without letting their hair become the main attraction.

Prayer

Gracious Father, I pray for wisdom to guide these girls. Help me show them how to take care of their hair without becoming obsessed by it. Thank You for allowing me to pass on knowledge of You. Amen.

Ponder

"Even the very hairs of your head are all numbered" (Matthew 10:30).

Preparation

- ✿ ask a hair dresser to come and talk with the girls about hair care
- ✿ a large mirror or stand-up makeup mirrors
- ✿ scrunchies or headbands
- ✿ extra makeup mirrors in case the girls forget or don't have any
- ✿ hairstyle magazines (borrow from hair salon)
- ✿ girls were asked to bring hair brushes and stand-up mirrors last week

❀ Ask two students ahead of time to role-play two girls. Tell them exaggeration is a lot of fun and helps make the point clearer to "the audience."

Frazzled Frieda's hair is always messy, unruly, sticking up, and looking like she forgot to comb or brush it in the morning.

Healthy Hair Harriet always has her hair combed and neat. Her hair shines and is nicely trimmed. She uses conditioner to keep her hair pretty and healthy.

Getting Started

"Welcome to class, girls! Let's open our time together with prayer."

Lead the girls in prayer, praising God for having everyone come to class and asking Him to help them discover more about themselves and serving Him.

"Last week you were asked to help people. Who would like to share what they did and how it felt?"

"We also worked on two verses. Our core memory verse from Colossians and either Proverbs 31:13 or 31:20. Who would like to recite for us?"

If no one recites, have them look up the verses and read them aloud.

Whatever you do, work at it with all your heart, as working for the Lord, not for men, since you know that you will receive an inheritance from the Lord as a reward. It is the Lord Christ you are serving (Colossians 3:24).

She selects wool and flax and works with eager hands (Proverbs 31:13).

She opens her arms to the poor and extends her hands to the needy (Proverbs 31:20).

"Today I want to introduce you to two girls, *Frazzled Frieda* and *Healthy Hair Harriet*."

Have Frazzled Frieda come loping into the room and wander around before sitting down.

"Frieda loves the wild look…or she just doesn't want to take the time to get her hair under control. She's always changing her hairstyle…although sometimes it's hard to tell because her hair is always messy, unruly, sticking up, and looking like she forgot to comb or brush it. Maybe she's afraid the comb will get stuck in her hair and be lost permanently. Her 'free' hair is the first and strongest impression people get when they see her." [Use hand quote marks when saying "free."]

Next have Healthy Hair Harriet walk serenely into the room and sit down.

"Healthy Hair Harriet, on the other hand, always has her hair combed and neat. Her hair shines, and she keeps it trimmed so split ends are kept at bay. She uses conditioner to keep her hair pretty and healthy. Although people notice her hair, it's her personality that stands out. Others assume that since she takes care with her grooming, she's a careful, responsible person."

Framing Your Face

Discussion   The student workbook has illustrations of various hairstyles and how they add or detract from a girl's face. Talk about the styles and different shapes of faces. Have the girls pull their hair back with scrunchies or headbands. Without embarrassing anyone, help the girls determine the shape of their faces and gently guide them to good hairstyles. Use hairstyle books and magazines to give them ideas or show them examples. This is a great time for the girls to interact with each other and you.

Keeping Hair Healthy

"What is the *mane* thing when it comes to your hair? Keeping it healthy and clean. So wash it regularly and use the right shampoo and conditioner:

- ✿ Normal hair needs normal shampoo and to be washed regularly.

- ✿ Oily hair gets greasy quickly so wash it daily.

- ✿ Dry hair is often coarse and curly. Use shampoo with moisturizer and don't wash it every day.

"What else should you do for your hair?

- ✿ Scrub your head thoroughly to clean the hair and massage your scalp, which helps keep hair roots healthy.

- ✿ Rinse hair well.

- ✿ Use hair conditioner.

- ✿ Use a comb on wet hair. Brushes will pull and break it.

- ✿ Brush your hair before bedtime to distribute the oil your hair follicles produce, which moisturizes your hair. It also stimulates your scalp.

- ✿ Staying hydrated and eating nutritious meals and snacks helps keep your hair healthy.

- ✿ Getting enough rest makes you—and your hair—healthier.

"Should we use a blow dryer or let our hair air dry? Blow drying dries out hair, so if you have a hairstyle that allows it, let your hair air dry. If you do blow dry, make sure you use conditioner. A blow dryer 'diffuser' is used usually for permed hair so the curls won't be blown out.

"Coloring also dries your hair out, so use extra conditioner if you decide to do this. Also check with your parents before you take the bold step of dyeing your hair.

"Hair texture varies from race to race. Caucasians' hair ranges from thin to thick, and comes in many colors. Some African-Americans have hair that curls tightly, while many Latinos and Asians have dark hair that is often straight. Certain types of hair need special care. Ask a hair specialist or hair dresser what he or she recommends for your hair type."

10 Tips for Happy Hair

❀ Keep hair clean.

❀ Brush it daily to distribute oil and make your hair shiny.

❀ Get hair trimmed every six weeks or so.

❀ Instead of fighting your hair type, work with it.

❀ If you have curly hair, enjoy those beautiful curls and find a style to show them off.

❀ Give your hair an oil treatment every one to two weeks if you have very dry hair.

❀ For frizzy hair, use lots of conditioner. You may need to use a styling product, such as gel or mousse.

❀ For limp hair, use a light volumizer.

❀ Wash oily hair daily, and lather up twice. Rinse with cool water.

❀ When you want hair off your neck, do pony tails, buns, or fancier hairdos. Check out your options.

A Special Activity

As a special treat, why not have an overnight at your house or at the church? Have the girls bring hair items and take turns experimenting with each other's hair. Bring beads, hair ties, hair combs, and anything else the girls can experiment with. You can even invite a hair specialist and a makeup artist to come and talk about their professions, their likes and dislikes, and to answer questions the girls may have.

 ## Reflecting Christ

"We've spent time learning how to take care of hair. But what's even more important is taking care of the treasure of our bodies. God gave us these bodies, and we want to keep them pure for Him. How? By following His guidelines for purity and morals.

"Today almost every TV show, movie, and stories in books have people hopping in out of bed with each other…even on the first or second date. Sexuality is presented as a pleasurable experience that has no long-term ties or effects on us. But there's more to sexual intimacy than the physical bond. A connection is made within and between both the man and woman in sexual relationships. Although some people can ignore this connection for a while, it catches up to them.

"Girls and women especially make emotional connections when sexuality is involved. That's one reason why God has set up marriage—so that two people can give themselves completely within the safety and assurance of lifelong commitment. I've known very few women who willingly engaged in premarital sex who haven't had huge regrets for not taking this aspect of their bodies more seriously and guarding it more carefully.

"And purity isn't just about sexuality. Here's an acrostic that may help you be more aware of God's plan when it comes to the vital area of our bodies:

Passion for Christ: We desire *purity* because our *passion* is for Christ and what He did on our behalf.

Unite: We seek to *unite* our desire with Christ's desire for our lives.

Repentant: We *repent* of our sins and turn our hearts to Christ.

Identity in Christ: Our *identity is in Christ* because God sent Him to earth for us, Jesus died for us, and the Holy Spirit came to live in us.

Transformed: We are being *transformed* into Christ's likeness as we seek Him through time spent in His Word, through prayer, and through study and meditation on God's principles and character.

Yielded: We *yield* our wills and desires to Him."

Schedule a personal time with each girl between now and the end of the charm course. Use this time to listen, answer any questions the girl may have regarding the various charm course areas, and talk about purity. This is an excellent opportunity to discuss any spiritual issues and present Christ as Savior and Helper.

June Hunt, founder of "Hope for the Heart," uses the "Four S" plan to share the gospel:

❀ God's purpose for each of us is *salvation*.

❀ The problem for each of us is *sin*.

❀ God's provision for each of us is the *Savior*.

❀ Our part is to *surrender*.

Feel free to use this…or one of the other easy-to-use sharing methods to reach out to your girls in this vital area. You can go to www.hopefortheheart.org for additional support in sharing the gospel and discussing purity.

7

Building a Foundation for Fashion
Developing a Classy Look

Purpose

To help the girls learn to build a wise foundation for fashion, and one that honors the Lord as well.

Prayer

Gracious Father, give me wisdom to help these lovely girls set their feet on the firm foundation of Your Word. Help me show them how to establish a foundation for fashion that honors You and serves them well for the jobs and projects You call them to. In Your Son's name I pray. Amen.

Ponder

"As God's chosen [women], holy and dearly loved, clothe yourselves with compassion, kindness, humility, gentleness and patience...and over all these virtues put on love, which binds them all together in perfect unity" (Colossians 3:12-14).

Preparation

- ✿ full-length mirror
- ✿ fashion magazines
- ✿ catalogs
- ✿ scissors
- ✿ whiteboard or chalkboard

✿ markers or chalk

✿ Read the "Styles, Shapes, and Colors" section carefully so you can bring in pictures and samples to illustrate the concepts and generate discussion.

✿ Introduce *Flawed-Fashion Felicia* and *Fashionable Fiona*.

> *Flawed-Fashion Felicia* should be wearing clashing stripes and squares and have some clothes too tight and some too loose. One item of clothing is ripped.

> *Fashionable Fiona* has well-coordinated clothes that fit. Her appearance is neat and everything is in good repair.

Getting Started

"Welcome, girls! Let's pray before we explore the amazing world of fashion."

Pray for your time together and that the girls and you will represent Christ to the people around you.

"Let's recite some of our memory verses."

Turn to the "Connecting with Christ" section and read the first three verses together.

"This week we're going to work on memorizing Philippians 4:13. Let's read it together.

"'I can do everything through him who gives me strength.'

"Memorize it and we'll recite it next week. Now, we have two special guests coming to class today."

You've asked each girl to walk into the classroom as you introduce them.

"Girls, here is *Flawed-Fashion Felicia*. Do you see anything about her appearance that could use some updating or changing?"

"I do. Her clothes are too tight in places and too big in others. They don't flatter her figure. And her clothes aren't in good repair.

"Here comes *Fashionable Fiona*. We can see right away that she cares about her appearance. What do you notice?"

"Yes, her clothes are coordinated and neat. They fit well and flatter her figure. She is neat and tidy and her clothes are in good repair."

The Comparison Game

"People come in a wide variety of shapes and sizes. Some are naturally round and short, while others are long and lean. Some are amply portioned while others are very thin. Unfortunately, few girls (and women) are satisfied with their figures. That's partly to do with our culture that worships various body shapes at different times, the negative messages advertisers tell us about our bodies so we'll buy their products, the body images presented in movies and books, and the subtle and not-so-subtle messages we pick up from those around us. Almost all females wish they could change one or more things about their bodies that God made.

"Fashion is an area where we tend to get caught up in comparing ourselves unfavorably with others. You've probably said, 'I wish I were tall like she is' or 'I wish my arms weren't so skinny.' Unfortunately, the world is constantly telling us how to look better and more appealing, subtly (and not so subtly) telling us that we don't look good and need help. This results in our discontent with what we look like…and then goes even deeper to our discontent with who we are. What a terrible deception!

"The lies are even more monumental when we realize the true secret to happiness is being content and confident in who we are, whose we are, and what our purpose on earth is (to please our heavenly Father).

"Yes, we secretly (and sometimes not so secretly) long to change our appearances. Our basic bone structures are here to stay, whether we like them or not, so we might as well accept them. This doesn't mean we can't enhance our looks though. With a few simple techniques we can emphasize our positive features and camouflage those we wish were different. We can alter the visual impression others get when they meet us.

"Girls, as we discuss our overall appearance, remember that God made us. We are wonderfully created. Culturally we may have a few flaws that we want to disguise to fit in better, but the 'core us' is beautiful."

Styles, Shapes, and Colors

"Have you noticed that one outfit will make you appear slim, while another makes you look chunky? Or that one dress seems to make you look shorter, while another makes you look taller? Your figure isn't changing, of course. It's the cut and style of the clothes that are making the difference.

 "What are some of the fashion guidelines you've learned so far from your mom and dad, your siblings, your friends, and from magazines and experts?"

Write down what the girls say on a whiteboard or chalkboard.

"Now let's see if we can figure out why some of these are true…and perhaps why a few aren't quite so true."

Why not bring in pictures and samples to illustrate these points? The girls will catch on faster, and your presentation will be more interesting.

"Four basic principles are involved when it comes to choosing clothes that flatter our shapes and make us presentable to the people around us.

"*Our eyes follow lines.* When people wear vertical stripes, our eyes give us a sense of height as we look up and down. When people wear horizontal stripes, our eyes move side to side, and we sense width. Vertical stripes emphasize height and deemphasize width, while horizontal lines deemphasize height and emphasize width.

"Our eyes are attracted to light colors. Because eyes are drawn to lighter colors first, wearing light colors on the parts of our bodies we want to emphasize and dark colors on what we want to minimize makes a huge difference. For large hips, wearing dark pants and light-colored tops draw attention away from the lower body.

"Our eyes are affected by comparative relationships. If one item is small while another is large, the difference is accentuated. If a large girl is carrying a small purse, we'll see the girl's size as larger and the purse's size as smaller. This carries over to print size too. If a tall girl is wearing a dress that has a soft and subtle checked pattern, she'll appear taller.

"Our eyes respond to proportion and balance. If we sense something out of balance we'll focus on pinpointing that instead of appreciating an overall look. If a girl is top heavy but very slender in the hips, she'll seem out of balance to us. In this case, by deemphasizing her top area and emphasizing her hips, she can make her body appear more balanced.

"Employing these basic principles involves intelligent scrutiny of our body shapes and clothes choices. But when we know we look good, and we feel good in what we wear, we gain confidence, are more active, and concentrate more on others.

"And here's the good news: We don't need a fabulous body to look good. The secret is knowing how to hide the parts we want to downplay and highlight the parts we love. Remember, we all struggle with our bodies. The goal is to present a consistent look from head to toe so our appearance looks like a unified whole rather than a collection of individual features. People's eyes will go to wherever there's a break in line, proportion, or balance. If a jacket hemline falls right where a person's hips are widest, her hips will look large. If the hemline falls a little higher up, say at the hipbone where the body is thinner, the eye sees and thinks 'slim.' "

The student workbook has tips and graphics that teach the girls how to look their best.

Savvy and Simple Suggestions

"Remember that our eyes notice proportion, so it's important to get clothes that match our body styles. A petite girl swamped by extra-long sweater sleeves or a curvy girl packed into a tight jacket says, 'Fashion Emergency!'

"Dressing well is playing up our good features and downplaying our not-so-good features. And tiny details can make a huge difference, which means we don't have to spend a lot of bucks or have a designer wardrobe to look our best. Here are some general tips.

- ✿ A low or wide neckline makes necks look longer and faces thinner. When necks look longer, the body looks slimmer.

- ✿ Avoid competing clothes. Emphasize one positive area at a time. If you're wearing a bright top, don't wear bright pants.

- ✿ Tops with elastic waists or made of stretchy fabric make tummies look larger.

❀ Thin people want to create curves, so wearing bulky clothes or layered clothes works wonderfully. Ruffles and pleats also work.

❀ Make sure undergarments fit well and are comfortable.

❀ Pantyhose should match the color of the skirt hem or the shoes.

Reflecting Christ

"Now that you've learned to emphasize the positive and camouflage the not-so-positives, let's turn our thoughts inward. We can be perfectly toned from head to toe and be dressed perfectly, but one quick flash of temper, one prideful toss of the head, one cutting remark can completely destroy the look we've worked hard to create. People will think, *She looks the part, but her heart isn't reflecting Jesus.* The sincere prayer of every girl who desires to be as lovely within as without is found in Psalm 139:23: '*Search me, O God, and know my heart; test me and know my anxious thoughts.*'

"The Lord is a master soul sculptor. His hand is deft; His touch is sure. Yield to Him as clay yields to the master potter. Deliberately let go of your hold on your life. When you are surrendered to Christ, God will take your life and make it pleasing and delightful in His sight."

Write from Your Heart

You can go over the questions with your girls or let them work on them at home and briefly discuss them next week.

8

Wardrobes That Work
Looking Your Best

Purpose

To teach the fundamentals of creating a wardrobe that is classy and conservative.

Prayer

Dear Jesus, may I always walk in wonder of You. Help me teach the girls with Your wisdom and love. Allow them to understand that the Holy Spirit lives inside them, and they are temples to You. In Your name I pray. Amen.

Ponder

"Clothe yourselves with humility toward one another, because, 'God opposes the proud but gives grace to the humble' " (1 Peter 5:5).

Preparation

✿ Ask two girls to role-play the girls you'll be introducing today.

Wacky Wilma, whose clothes always look like she dressed hurriedly, picked clothes up off her floor to put on. Her clothes are in need of repair.

Tailored Tina has it all together, and she looks it. Her outfit is well coordinated, everything matches—even her shoes—her hair is neat and tidy. Her clothes are wrinkle free and look clean. They are in excellent condition without any rips or repairs.

❧ chalkboard or whiteboard and writing implements

❧ color swatches big enough to help the girls discover the "colors" that bring out their best looks (see "Find Your Best Colors" section)

❧ consider inviting a colorist to explain colors and drape a few girls

❧ outfits and accessories of various colors and styles to mix and match with good *and* bad results (see "Finding Your Best Colors" section)

Getting Started

"I'm so glad you made it to class. Today we're going to discuss our wardrobes and how to dress for success in several areas. But let's dedicate our time to God first."

Lead the girls in prayer.

"Let's recite our memory verse—Philippians 4:13. Who wants to give it a shot?"

I can do everything through him who gives me strength.

 "Two new girls are joining our class today: *Wacky Wilma* and *Tailored Tina*. How would you describe them?"

Write down their insights on a chalkboard or whiteboard. Discuss and direct the conversation to bring out these traits:

❧ *Wacky Wilma:* looks "thrown together," wrinkled and soiled clothing, tattered and torn garments

❧ *Tailored Tina* looks "put together," clean and tidy clothing, tailored and tasteful garments

"People form their ideas about who we are by the clues we furnish through the clothes we wear and our attitudes. So let's not send out false signals by wearing boring outfits or looking unkempt. Clothes don't necessarily 'make the girl,' but whether we like it or not, they do serve as a 'labeling device.' What we wear affects how people relate to us."

Secrets of Style

"We don't need a lot of cash to shop with or an overflowing closet to dress well. So what's the secret of great style? *The desire to look our best.* We can develop a great sense of style, good taste in clothes, and a game plan for dressing nicely and yet inexpensively. Here are some basic principles.

"*Choose classic styles.* Have two or three of the basic styles, such as well-made pants, skirts, blouses, jeans, dresses, and sweaters. (Trends come and go, but classics stay forever...or close to it.) Spice up the basics with inexpensive belts, scarves, sunglasses, and jewelry.

"*Learn to sew.* If you're not handy with a needle and thread, find someone to teach you. A tuck here, a dart there, or a new hemline can cleverly change an entire look without too much cost. An ankle-length summer dress could morph into a tea-length dress that looks nice with dress shoes.

"*Avoid extremes.* Swim down the middle of the fashion stream by not wearing the longest, shortest, fullest, or slimmest of anything. A moderate approach enables you to wear clothes longer and still be in fashion.

"*Dress to reflect your personality.* You are a special, unique person. Many teens don't want to dress differently than their peers, and a certain amount of conformity is desirable or we'll come across as trying too hard or not trying hard enough. But we can add personal touches to make each look our own. So let's dress to express *our* personalities. Our clothes should reflect us.

"*Dare to be you.* Be genuine. We need to choose clothes that look becoming on *us*, styles that flatter *our* figures, colors that enhance *our* skin tones, and trends that spotlight *our* good points. Let's embrace who we are and what our best styles are. If we're on the dainty side, we shouldn't dress like an All-American in field hockey. If we're sports-minded and athletic, we shouldn't try to force ourselves into dainty mode. We can use our imaginations and wear clothes with a flair that makes them our own...that creates our signature style. We're brave enough to be ourselves, right? Right!

"*Dressing appropriately.* We want to show up at every event dressed appropriately, which means paying attention to the style of the event, dressing modestly, and being tasteful. For example, when going to a wedding, most people wouldn't wear white. And people would think we're strange if we turned up at a beach party or mountain picnic in prom dresses."

A Quick Style Guide

Discussion — "Let's brainstorm some general guidelines for what to wear to certain events, places, and occasions. When we're done, you can note this in your workbook and make a photocopy to post on the inside of your closet door for reference. And remember, what is appropriate for one girl may not be appropriate for another. And let's stay positive. We want to ask three questions for each situation:

✿ Is the apparel appropriate for the occasion?

✿ Is the choice of coordinates, accessories, and such in good taste?

✿ How do the choices change depending on the girl's body type and personality?"

Cover the four main areas (church, school, co-ed party, dinner out). If you choose, cover additional events, depending on the time available. Write on a chalkboard or whiteboard the guidelines the girls and you come up with. Since there is quite a bit of information and we don't want the girls to have to write too much, you could compile the list at home and bring copies next week for the girls to keep for reference.

Church: _____

_____

School: _____

_____

Friend's co-ed birthday party: _____

_____

Dinner at a fancy restaurant: _____

_____

Optional discussion suggestions

Activities such as bowling, skating, skiing: _____

_____

Art venues (symphony, an opera or play, musicals, ballet): _____

_____

A contemporary music concert: _____

_____

A wedding: _____

_____

An outdoor church meeting: _____

_____

A Christian camp: _____

_____

A job interview: _____

_____

Meeting parents' bosses or coworkers: _____

_____

Dressing with Simplicity

"Keep your clothes and accessories simple. Don't pile on the jewelry and colors. Remember to have only one attention grabber. If you wear a shimmering dress, make the belt a low-key accessory."

Mixing and Matching

Discussion Using the outfits you brought, have the girls discuss which tops go with which bottoms and how they would mix and match. Point out the conflicts between pattern types and vivid colors. Detail what looks vibrant and what looks dull.

Finding Your Best Colors

"Girls, colors can really make your eyes sparkle and your face glow. Or they can make you look tired and washed out. How do we find out which colors look the best on us? Trial and error, opinions offered by family and friends, and what we think. We also often naturally gravitate to colors that look good on us.

"We'll do color draping in class today. We'll also look at several outfits and accessories to see what looks good and what doesn't. This is going to be fun!"

Use color swatches to drape the girls. If you have a guest colorist, have him or her share recommendations. Also use the various outfits for color and matching too. Make sure some items clash so the "not so good" looks can be shown and discussed.

What Clothes Do You Have?

"Most of us have so many clothes we don't even know what we have. We've outgrown some clothes but kept them around. We have clothes we never wear because we don't like them. And then there are the clothes we hoped would fit…but didn't or looked odd on us.

"A great step in wardrobe management is to go through your clothes and eliminate the ones you no longer wear or that don't fit well. Thrift stores, missions, and family shelters love to get clothes that are in good shape."

"There are some basic questions to ask as you pull each item from your dresser or closet. As we go through these, write the details down in your workbooks for reference when you get home and sort through your clothes.

✿ *Does it fit?* If it almost fits or might if you lose weight, don't keep it.

✿ *Will I wear it in the next year?* If the answer is no, don't keep it.

✿ *Do I like it?* If not, give it away.

- ✿ *Is it out of style?* It may be out of style for you, but not for someone else. Give it away.

- ✿ *Does it fill a need for a special occasion?* Is it dressy for a special occasion you may attend, such as a wedding? If yes, keep it.

- ✿ *When was the last time I wore it?* If it's been a year, get rid of it.

- ✿ *Does it make me look good?* If not really or only maybe, give it away.

"After you give away those clothes, go through your clothes and create a simple inventory of what you have. This will help you know what's available for mixing and matching, and also let you know if there are basic items you need to get."

Reflecting Christ

Read the student workbook's "Reflecting Christ" section and discuss modesty, appropriate attire, and perhaps touch on how a girl's look may affect boys. Emphasize that girls want to dress modestly and with class because they represent Christ. While they are not responsible for boys' behaviors, they are responsible for the way they are dressed. However, girls should be aware that society puts much of the burden of sexual restraint on females. Our culture stresses that boys are visual creatures, but in reality both boys and girls are visual, so we need to be aware of what we're wearing. That said, girls should be modest and aware of how they're dressing and how their look and actions affect others. They're also representing God and His standards.

"Girls, clothing choice is very personal and yet can have a strong impact on those around us. We want to make sure we stay modest and appropriate. I know this subject can get a little embarrassing, but modesty is important and how we dress reflects our values and how much we value God's principles. So let's consider some specific situations.

"Say you're at a party and wearing a fairly short skirt. What happens when you drop something and lean over to pick it up? How much of your legs will show because your skirt will naturally rise up as you bend over?

"Or how much of your bodice shows if your shirt or blouse is low-cut and you lean over from your desk to pick up a pencil?

"When your jeans are very tight, especially if they are low-rise jeans, what view do the people around get as you walk, stand, sit, and lean over?

"Modesty isn't always respected in our culture today, but it's a core value that honors God's principles, helps us (and others) avoid temptation, and highlights how we treasure the bodies God created for us."

You could have women come into the class at this point to reveal what happens when clothes are immodest...even "slightly" immodest. Make sure these "volunteers" don't embarrass easily. It's probably best not to use girls from the class; college-age women would work well.

Make this entire section a gentle, thoughtful, circumspect discussion. Keep evenhanded about sexuality for boys and girls.

Write from Your Heart

This is a good opportunity to review modesty with the girls and have a discussion about clothing. Go over the questions in class or have them do them at home and briefly touch on them next week (a second opportunity to go over this important area).

9

Completing Your Look
Letting Your Personality Shine

Purpose

To teach the basic principles of grooming and organization so personalities shine through.

Prayer

Gracious God, I'm so glad You like things orderly. Help me show the girls how organization can enhance their lives and their walk with You. In your Son's name I pray. Amen.

Ponder

"Everything should be done in a fitting and orderly way" (1 Corinthians 14:40).

Preparation

❀ Invite someone who is gifted in organization to be a guest speaker on how to organize closets, purses, and school materials in a practical and fun way.

❀ Create a checklist for what needs to be done before leaving the house. See "Before Leaving the House" in the "Details Add Up" section.

❀ Ask two students to role-play this week's characters.

> *Sloppy Serena* looks like her clothes, accessories, hairdo, and everything else was done hastily and with little thought. She's frantic because she can't find anything in her purse and came to class without her notebook or pen because they were lost.

Together Torina is organized and calm. She can find anything in her purse quickly because she has compartments and small bags that organize everything. Her look is neat and tidy. She is prepared for class.

Getting Started

"Welcome! We're going to discover how to get organized today, but first let's dedicate this time to God."

Pray for the girls, the class, and your teaching.

"First let's look at our fifth core verse. Turn to the 'Connecting with Christ' section, and let's read Colossians 3:12-14 together. It's long, but I know we can get this memorized too!

> " 'Therefore, as God's chosen people, holy and dearly loved, clothe yourselves with compassion, kindness, humility, gentleness and patience. Bear with each other and forgive whatever grievances you may have against one another. Forgive as the Lord forgave you. And over all these virtues put on love, which binds them all together in perfect unity.'

"Work on this verse this week, and we'll go over it again next week. By now you know we're all unique individuals, and we all have interesting and wonderful personalities.

"Today I'd like you to meet *Sloppy Serena*."

Have Sloppy Serena enter the room. Invite discussion about her overall look.

"Now here comes *Together Torina*."

Have Torina enter the room and discuss her overall look.

"Our personalities affect how we embrace everything we do. We are fearfully and wonderfully made by God for His purposes. How we are is God's gift to us. What we do with His gift is our gift back to Him. Here's a simple, layperson's guide to four basic personality types. As we go through these, write the characteristics in your workbook."

❀ *Get-it-done Donna:* Donna is a take-charge person who is good at organizing things...and people...to get tasks done.

❀ *Fun-loving Felicia:* Great fun to have around, Felicia is very social and wants to be with people all the time. She does tend to forget details a lot.

✿ *Peaceful Phyllis:* An easygoing, go-with-the-flow person, Phyllis is a peacemaker who gets along with everyone…and wants everyone else to do the same.

✿ *Conscientious Connie:* Connie is dependable and responsible. She does her best and tends to be a perfectionist. She worries about not getting tasks done right.

"Most people are a combination of personality types, but one aspect is more dominant. Which personality do you most closely resemble?"

For the next section, please see the student workbook.

Details Add Up

"Girls, hygiene is important. When people hit their teens, hormones hit and our bodies go through many changes. We start sweating more and body odor becomes an issue. Our skin becomes more oily in places, and we break out more often."

A Fresh Start or a Great Finish

"We need to take showers or baths frequently. Although we don't usually need to take them every day for cleanliness (unless we have gym or do physical work), in our culture many people do to start their days refreshed and energized.

"Keeping our hair clean and shiny, our skin healthy, and smelling nice are small details, but we've all come into contact with people who let one or more of these slide for one reason or another, and they weren't pleasant to be around. Our appearance says a lot about how we feel about ourselves. Another reason to take care of our bodies is because God created them."

Before Leaving the House

"Have you ever noticed someone whose shirt isn't buttoned correctly, whose pants have a big rip, or who has on one brown shoe and one black shoe? It happens. To avoid embarrassment, before you leave the house take a quick spin in front of a full-length mirror. Check:

✿ Is my belt threaded through each loop?

✿ Is my shirt tucked in all the way around?

✿ Is my bra showing?

✿ Is the clothing label tucked under the neckline?

✿ Is the center seam of my skirt off center?

✿ Is every button buttoned and my zipper zipped?

"What else should we check for?"

✿ _____

✿ _____

✿ _____

✿ _____

"One way to make sure everything is in place before you head out is to make a checklist or chart and post it on your bedroom door."

You can make a sample checklist as a visual if you'd like. (The following chart is in the student workbook.)

My "To Do" List

Daily	Weekly	Monthly
Shower or bath	Manicure nails	Hair trimmed
Wash hair	Care for feet	(every 6 weeks)
Brush hair and style	Clean out purse and	Breast self-exam
Brush and floss teeth	backpack	Clean shoes
(morning & night)	Check clothing:	
Wash face and moisturize	• launder	
(morning & night)	• iron	
Shaving (every 2 or 3 days)	• cleaners	
Deodorant	• repair	
Lotion	• put away properly	
Clean nails	• select for this week	
Drink water (6-8 glasses)		
Exercise		
8 hours of sleep minimum		
Healthy breakfast		
Healthy lunch		
Healthy dinner		
Healthy snacks		
Wash hands often		
Check clothes in mirror		
before leaving the house		

Personality Profile

 "Remember when we discussed personalities in chapter 9? There was:

❀ *Get-it-done Donna:* Donna is a take-charge person who is good at organizing things…and people…to get tasks done.

❀ *Fun-loving Felicia:* Great fun to have around, Felicia is very social and wants to be with people all the time. She may forget details at times.

❀ *Peaceful Phyllis:* An easygoing, go-with-the-flow person, Phyllis is a peacemaker who gets along with everyone…and wants everyone else to do the same.

❀ *Conscientious Connie:* Connie is dependable and responsible. She does her best and tends to be a perfectionist. She worries about not getting tasks done right.

"If friends called up and asked these girls to go to the mall, how might they go about getting ready?

"*Get-it-done Donna* is organized. She has a place for everything, and everything is in its place. She can find the clothes she wants to wear and the accessories to go with them. But she's thinking about playing tennis instead of going to the mall with some of her friends.

"*Fun-loving Felicia* is eagerly looking forward to seeing her friends. She can't wait to get to school to visit…but where did she put the house key and her billfold? They must be in one of the piles on the floor.

"*Peaceful Phyllis* is calm and prepared. She's been ready to go for quite a while and is using the 'extra' time to pray for some friends who were bickering. She asks God to intercede and help her friends work out their differences.

"*Conscientious Connie* heaves a big sigh. What will her friends be wearing? She wants to fit in and wear something similar. She's just tried on her fourth outfit…and now it's time to go and she's not quite ready.

"Which girl do you relate to most?"

"Personality plays a huge role in how we organize, how we get ready for the day, how we work through the day, and how we end the day. So as you get ready, take into consideration your 'natural bent,' and adjust. If you tend to be messy, get more organized and establish a specific place to put your keys and billfold. If you are more like *Conscientious Connie,* get up earlier so you have more time. It's much easier to work *with* yourself than against yourself."

Time to Get Personal

BO and You

"Teens and adults sweat (perspire) and have to deal with body odor (BO). That's a fact of life. Odor becomes a problem we must deal with when we turn 11 or 12 and continues until we get to meet Jesus face-to-face.

"Thankfully there are many deodorants to choose from. You can get cream, clear, liquid, spray, gel, and solids. Find one you like and that works with your body. *Use it every day.* Deodorant comes in scented and unscented. If you get scented, make sure it doesn't clash with your favorite perfume or body wash."

To Shave or Not to Shave?

"In our society women and teenage girls usually shave under their arms and their legs. This is mostly for aesthetics, although underarm hair does trap sweat, which can contribute to body odor. Some teens and women also shave their bikini lines for swimming.

"I recommend you talk to your moms about shaving. It's easiest to shave in the bathtub because water helps the razor move smoothly without scraping the skin. Never use an electric razor in the bathtub or you might get electrocuted and even die. Shaving cream or lotion also helps the razor move smoothly over your skin. After shaving your legs, apply body lotion."

Up Close and Personal

"One unavoidable problem is bad breath. And if we eat strong-tasting foods, such as garlic bread and onions, our breath can even make people gag. To counter this problem, there are quite a few options. Brushing your teeth with toothpaste helps eliminate bacteria and other odor-producing substances. Breath mints and gum are good on-the-go solutions. Using mouth wash every morning and before big events is a good preventative measure."

A Touch of Fragrance

"Perfume or colognes add a subtle allure. Use scents sparingly because a little goes a long way. These products aren't meant to cover body odor. Perfume is an *enhancement.* Perfumes and colognes can be very expensive, so shop within your budget. There are many scents to choose from, so you're sure to find some you like at a reasonable cost.

"Quite a few people are allergic to perfumes these days, which is another reason to go easy on the amount. Too much perfume can be as bad as not taking a shower for a month, so be conservative."

Is Your Clothing Neat and Clean?

"Now that you've taken care of your body, let's move on to taking care of your clothes. Make sure every garment you put on is clean. Before donning your clothes, inspect every piece:

- ✿ Is the collar dirty?
- ✿ Are the cuffs clean?
- ✿ Is the neckline soiled?
- ✿ Is the belt dirty?
- ✿ Do the armholes have perspiration stains?
- ✿ Are there any food spots or other stains?

"Clothes need to be cleaned. The cleaning instructions are on the labels. Check them carefully. Some clothes are dry clean only, some are hand wash, some say don't use bleach, and some say wash in cold water only. Follow the label instructions carefully.

"If clothing needs repaired, take care of it right away. If you don't know how to sew, ask your mom to teach you. Until then, ask if she'll repair any rips or holes. If a button is loose, take care of it quickly so you don't lose it.

"When you take your clothes off, hang them up or put them in the dirty clothes hamper. Because washing is hard on fabrics, unless you've gotten an item of clothes dirty or smelly, don't wash it after each use.

"Hanging clothes up helps prevent wrinkles."

If the Shoe Fits

"Make sure your shoes are in good condition:

- ❁ Are they scuffed?
- ❁ Are the heels worn down?
- ❁ Are the laces broken or dirty?
- ❁ If leather, are they dull and need polishing?

"One secret to making shoes last is to let them air out between uses. Having two pair so you can alternate every day is terrific."

Being a Bag Lady

"Purses can be so handy. You can carry your makeup, billfold, fingernail clippers, a mini toothbrush and toothpaste, and more. But carrying a heavy purse is bad for your shoulders so be reasonable about what you put in there…and clean it often. Purses seem to accumulate items on their own!

"For organizing, buy purses that have pockets on the inside. Or purchase or make small bags to keep makeup and other related items in. Another option is to use Ziploc baggies. Keeping makeup and products that may leak or spill in plastic or plastic-lined bags is a good idea, plus it makes them easier to find. Periodically wipe down the inside and outside of your purse."

Reflecting Christ

"The Bible tells us to be strong in the Lord and in His mighty power. As we're getting ready in the morning and 'Completing Our Look,' let's make sure we have on the armor of God. We're getting our outer selves ready, and we need to have our spiritual selves ready too. We need time for prayer and to be in the Word to keep us strong.

"Ephesians 6 warns us that there will be spiritual attacks. The enemy (Satan) will try to discourage us, hurt our character, find ways to keep us from walking with the Lord, and tempt us with the ways of the world. Victory over Satan comes through Jesus, and we pray in His name to help us throughout the day. Who will look up and read Ephesians 6:13-18 for us?"

Put on the full armor of God, so that when the day of evil comes, you may be able to stand your ground, and after you have done everything, to stand. Stand firm then, with the belt of truth buckled around your waist, with the breastplate of righteousness in place, and with your feet fitted with the readiness that comes from the gospel of peace. In addition to all this, take up the shield of faith, with which you can extinguish all the flaming arrows of the evil one. Take the helmet of salvation and the sword of the Spirit, which is the word of God. And pray in the Spirit on all occasions with all kinds of prayers and requests. With this in mind, be alert and always keep on praying for all the saints.

"Let's break down into steps how we can put on the armor God provides every morning. Thelma Wells offers a great routine in her book *Don't Give In, God Wants You to Win!*:

✿ As you put on your panties, pants, or belt, say 'God, I am putting on my *belt of truth*. Help me to be truthful and to stand for Your truth today.'

✿ As you put on your bra, pray, 'Lord, I put on my *breastplate of righteousness*. I'm trusting You to protect my heart from the enemy. Help me make the right choices today.'

✿ As you put on your shoes, pray, 'God, I have my *feet* fitted with the readiness that comes from the gospel of peace. Help me to walk in Your ways today.'

✿ As you put on your shirt (blouse or dress), say, 'Lord, I'm taking up my *shield of faith* to knock away the flaming arrows sent by the evil one. Thank You for protecting me from the enemy.'

✿ As you brush your hair, say out loud, 'Here's my *helmet of salvation* because I trust You, Jesus, as my Lord and Savior. You are with me every minute of every day, and I praise and thank You.'

✿ When you gather your purse or backpack, proclaim, 'I'm armed with the *sword of the Spirit*, which is the Word of God. I'm ready. Guide me and use me today for Your kingdom, Lord.' "

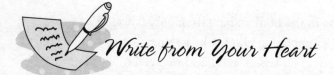

Write from Your Heart

Go over the questions in the student workbook. You can have the girls answer them at home and discuss them briefly at the beginning of the next class if you'd like.

10

Excellence in Etiquette
Gracefulness at the Table

Purpose

To take the "after" pictures see chapter 1. Also teach the girls the importance of etiquette, table manners, introductions, and being a young lady with *class*.

Prayer

Dear God, please give these girls sensitive hearts to honor other people's needs before their own. Help them see that good manners are important. Be with me as I teach. In Your Son's name I pray. Amen.

Ponder

"So in everything, do to others what you would have them do to you" (Matthew 7:12).

Preparation

❀ set up the picture-taking per instructions in chapter 1.

❀ glue

❀ various table settings and napkins to show how to set the table properly, how to pass food, use multiple utensils properly, and demonstrate table etiquette

❀ food to help with manners, such as french fries and grapes (see "Fingers, Forks, and Foods")

❀ whiteboard or chalkboard and markers or chalk

❀ table for two that includes a snack plate with a cupcake and some other foods that require using utensils

✿ ask two girls to role-play this week

> *Rude Rudi* walks in while snacking…maybe tossing peanuts into her mouth. (She can spill a couple without noticing.) Have her plop down at the table, slouching as she says she hates apples and grabs the only cupcake. She chows down, talking while she's eating. Have her burp and then laugh.

> During Rude Rudi's time, have *Mannerly Molly* walk in and sit down. She puts her napkin in her lap and asks Rudi if she'd like some apple slices (or whatever). Then she daintily eats, but doesn't eat all the food. She keeps her mouth closed while chewing.

Getting Started

"Hi, Girls! Are you ready to get started? Let's open our time with prayer."

Pray for your girls and that class time be productive and helpful.

"Who will recite Philippians 4:8 for us today?"

> *Finally, [sisters], whatever is true, whatever is noble, whatever is right, whatever is pure, whatever is lovely, whatever is admirable—if anything is excellent or praiseworthy—think about such things.*

"Now who will recite 2 Corinthians 5:17?"

> *If anyone is in Christ, he is a new creation, the old has gone, the new has come!*

"Very good.

Checking Your Progress

"Today we're going to take the 'after' pictures to compare with the pictures we took when we worked on chapter one."

Carefully following the instructions in chapter 1, set up the classroom for taking the "after pictures." Take the pictures, pass out the after photos, and note if there has been general improvement. Have the girls glue their photos in chapter 1 after the "Before" pictures and above the "After" photo caption.

"Okay. Let's move on to etiquette.

Today we have two new characters to meet."

Have *Rude Rudi* burst into the room and go to the table and play her part. After a minute or so, have *Mannerly Molly* enter and play her part. When they're done, open a discussion.

 "One girl is named *Mannerly Molly*, and one girl is called *Rude Rudi*. Which girl is which, and what differences did you notice?"

If you'd like, you can point out other unmannerly behaviors and have the girls act them out as you talk.

The "G Rule"

Discussion "How many of you have heard of 'The Golden Rule'? Did you know it comes from the Bible? It's found in Matthew 7:12: *'So in everything, do to others what you would have them do to you.'* How does this apply to our daily lives? Well, you wouldn't want someone to come up to you at school and kick your shins, so under the Golden Rule, you wouldn't do that to someone else.

"But let's take the 'G Rule' further. How can we apply it to having good manners at the table? Without getting personal or pointing fingers, what are some things you've seen people do that annoy you? For instance, one person I know hates it when people smack their gum. Let's make a list."

Use a whiteboard or chalkboard and note what the girls share.

"When we see annoying habits, the first thing to ask is, 'Do I do this?' No one enjoys sitting at a nice restaurant and listening to the people at the next table arguing, treating the waiters rudely, or talking loudly on their cell phones. And sitting at the breakfast table at home when people are all talking at once… or perhaps no one is talking at all, can be quite uncomfortable. When family or friends are gathered, answering your cell phone or texting is disrespectful. It tells the people you're with that they aren't very important or they're boring (which may be true, but it's inappropriate to tell them or imply it). Phone calls can wait, so turn off your phone before meals. Following the 'G Rule' in manners means avoiding habits and actions that may annoy, disrespect, or gross out fellow diners.

"And what about when we're alone? Can we toss out the rules then? The key is 'reasonableness.' Generally, good manners should be practiced always so they become second nature. We don't want to have to concentrate on making sure we're looking good and acting good when we're dining and visiting with others. On the other hand, when we're eating alone, making ourselves sit at a table set with fancy silverware, cloth napkins, and water goblets may be overkill. But we want to practice good table manners because if they're natural to us we can relax and enjoy eating with others.

"Another good reason to develop good manners is that more and more businesses are conducting interviews in restaurants. Potential employers believe they can get a lot of information by the way we eat—and they're right. If we're very sloppy, talk with our mouths full, or demand extra service from the waiter, they may discern we're careless or too picky and hard to work with. Finding a job may not be in your near future, but it's not far off. Show respect for the people you're with and practice good manners. They'll notice.

"What are some guidelines for good manners?"

The Meal

Note: The bulleted information is in student workbook under "Review," before "Reflecting Christ."

"Eating a 'family style' meal is a team effort. People are passing food around, serving themselves from dishes, and enjoying conversation. When we follow good manners, the meal is smooth, fun, and fair. If we make up our own rules as we go along, others won't be ready or know what to do. This causes confusion, spills, and awkward situations. Using good manners also shows consideration to others because it helps them know what to do. What are some great guidelines for sharing a meal?"

Before the Meal

❀ If you're going to be 10 to 15 minutes late, call the host.

❀ When approaching the table, wait for your host to tell you where to sit.

❀ Never sit at a table until the host does, unless instructed.

❀ Don't make negative comments about the food or table presentation.

❀ If you don't like something, keep it to yourself. Speak only positive, praising words to your host about the food, service, and his or her hard work.

Being Seated

❀ If offered, allow a gentleman to seat you. He will pull out your chair. Lower yourself carefully, keeping your back straight. Don't bend forward. After you're seated, you may wish to stand slightly to allow the gentleman to slide your chair a little closer to the table.

❀ If the gentleman doesn't offer to seat you (or open a car door), don't demand it or say something rude. Some boys and men haven't been taught this etiquette.

❀ Don't crowd someone's leg space. Keep your feet pulled back just in front of your chair. Keep your knees together. Remember, there are twice as many feet and legs under the table as there are heads above.

❀ Make sure you don't elbow your neighbors. Keep your elbows close to your body.

❀ If you must blow your nose, excuse yourself from the table and find the restroom.

✿ Sit straight but relaxed. Keep your hands in your lap when not using them. Don't lean over your plate or bob your head down when taking a bite of food.

When Food Is Served

✿ Note which way the host passes food and follow his or her lead.

✿ Make sure you pass on food that is passed to you.

✿ Never put your own silverware into a serving dish.

✿ Don't make any negative comments about the food or food choices.

✿ Don't reach across someone's plate for an item. Ask for it to be passed to you. Remember to say thank you.

✿ When taking food, take what's closest to you. Don't search for the "best" piece.

✿ Take a moderate portion of food, and don't take more than you will eat. Don't leave food on your plate.

✿ When choosing silverware, always start from the outside and move inward. For instance, if there is a salad fork and a dinner fork, the salad fork will be on the outside because salad is usually the first course. The next course is dinner, so the dinner fork will be next to the plate.

At the Table

✿ Don't talk with your mouth full.

✿ Don't use your fingers to push food onto your silverware. Use another utensil.

✿ Drink quietly and in small sips. If you dribble, discreetly wipe your mouth with your napkin.

✿ If unsure about liking a certain food, try it. If you don't like it, swallow it or quietly take it out of your mouth the same way it went in and place it back on your plate.

✿ Don't use your fingers except with specific foods. Use your utensils to cut food into smaller bites and move food on your plate.

✿ If you spill food, quietly excuse yourself and clean yourself off in the bathroom. If you spill on someone else, offer the person your napkin and then get more towels if necessary. If the spill is unobtrusive and doesn't affect anyone, ignore it until after dinner. If the spill might stain the floor or tablecloth, quietly tell the host.

✿ If you drop a utensil, quietly ask for a clean one. Pick up the dropped one after the meal.

✿ Don't start eating until everyone has their food unless instructed otherwise.

✿ Use your napkins, not your clothes.

✿ Avoid distasteful, disgusting, or questionable subjects, such as disasters, illness, horror movies, medical conditions, body functions, and garbage.

✿ Pace your eating by observing the plates of those around you. Don't eat too fast or too slow. People may feel rushed if they're still eating when you're finished, and you don't want to delay a meal while people wait for you. Cut down on talking or talk more, as appropriate.

✿ Make an effort to talk to everyone at the table, if possible. If there are many guests, talk to those in your area.

✿ Thank the cook and/or host.

You can call on the girls for each scenario to encourage group participation. They can either give the answer or you can act out the answer.

"Okay, girls, now let's have some fun. Remember *Rude Rudi* and *Mannerly Molly?* Let's figure out how they'd handle these situations.

"*Situation 1:* Rude Rudi is going to be 20 minutes late for dinner because band practice got out late. When she arrives home, the family is just heading into the dining room for dinner.

"Now imagine Rudi standing on the football field after band practice. What does she do? For instance, she might mention to her friends that she's late, but then stands around and talks to them anyway. What else?"

Make sure these items are covered:

✿ Finally puts her instrument away and heads home, calling a friend on her cell to talk about the cute trombone player.

✿ Ignores her mom's reminder to wash her hands.

✿ Pushes past her brother to get into the dining room first.

✿ Says "Yuck!" when she sees that squash is the vegetable.

✿ Immediately sits down and starts eating while everyone else is getting settled.

✿ Dominates the conversation by going on and on about her day.

✿ Blows her nose at the table.

"Now, let's look at the same scenario with Mannerly Molly. What happens?"

You'll want to make sure these are covered:

✿ She calls her mom as soon as band practice is over to explain why she's late and when she'll get home.

✿ Puts her instrument away and heads straight home.

✿ Washes her hands when she arrives and chats with her family while they gather for dinner.

✿ Sits with the rest of the family and comments on the delicious food that was prepared.

✿ Listens as others share about their day and asks questions to show her interest in them.

✿ Shares highlights of what happened in her day.

✿ Excuses herself to go blow her nose, and then rejoins the table without announcing nose-blowing details.

"Which girl would you like to have dinner with? Which girl helps make dinner a pleasant experience for everyone?"

"*Scenario 2:* Rude Rudi is at the table with her family and some guests her parents invited. The food is being passed around and everyone is talking. What could Rude Rudi be doing to live up to her name? For instance, someone passed her the potatoes. She took some, put the potato platter by her plate, and started eating. What else do you think she'd be doing?"

Have the students answer/act out what's happening.

"Now, let's look at the same scenario with Mannerly Molly. What happens?"

Have the students answer/act out what's happening.

"*Scenario 3:* Everyone at the table has their food. Conversation is lively, and everyone seems to be having a good time. What will Rude Rudi do next?"

Have the students answer/act out what's happening.

"Now, let's look at the same scenario with Mannerly Molly. What happens?"

Have the students answer/act out what's happening.

Feel free to do more of these exercises, drawing on the lists for scenarios.

Fingers, Forks, and Food (This section is not in the student workbook.)

Show your girls how to eat the following foods gracefully and with good manners.

- ✿ fresh fruit (fingers)
- ✿ pickles, radishes, olives (fingers)
- ✿ french fries—dinner fork at a dinner, fingers when eating informally
- ✿ corn on the cob (fingers using corn holders)
- ✿ pudding, custard, ice cream (teaspoon)
- ✿ fried chicken (knife, fork, and fingers)
- ✿ hot sandwiches (knife and fork)
- ✿ regular sandwiches (fingers)
- ✿ cake (salad or dessert fork)
- ✿ celery or carrot sticks (fingers)
- ✿ nuts or mints (fingers)
- ✿ cantaloupe (teaspoon)
- ✿ seafood cocktail (oyster fork)
- ✿ buttering corn on the cob (knife)
- ✿ buttering baked potato (fork)
- ✿ buttering bread or roll (butter knife or dinner knife)

There are some special details you'll want to teach the girls in your class.

"What is the proper way to butter bread at the dinner table?

✿ hold the bread slightly above the plate

✿ break off a small section

✿ butter one portion and eat it

"Is there a proper way to eat soup?

✿ use a soup spoon

✿ traditionally speaking, dip the spoon in by moving it away from your body. You can also dip the spoon normally, but avoid the 'shoveling food into your mouth' look

✿ sip from the side of the spoon to avoid spills

✿ hold large crackers in your hand, but put oyster crackers in the soup

"What do we do with pits or seeds from fruit?

✿ If you need to take any food from your mouth, do it the same way it went in. If you used a fork, discreetly spit the food onto the fork and put it on the side of your plate.

"What about table mistakes?

✿ If silverware is dropped, leave it on the floor until after the meal. Ask for a new one.

✿ If food is spilled and it is causing no harm, ignore it until after the meal. If it might stain the carpet or tablecloth, discreetly clean it up. If spilled on another person, immediately offer your napkin and apologize."

A Fun Little Quiz

Going over the quiz in the student workbook together might be fun for you and the girls. Or you can have them answer the questions and review the answers next week. The student workbook includes this: "*Note:* Your teacher will go over these with you and supply the correct answers."

Reflecting Christ

Have one of the girls read 1 Corinthians 13:4-8:

Love is patient, love is kind. It does not envy, it does not boast, it is not proud. It is not rude, it is not self-seeking, it is not easily angered, it keeps no record of wrongs. Love does not delight in evil but rejoices with the truth. It always protects, always trusts, always hopes, always perseveres. Love never fails.

Now have the girls paraphrase it using courtesy or manners in place of love. For example:

> Courtesy is thoughtful and kind. It never embarrasses others or makes them appear awkward. It thinks of others first and self last. It doesn't steal the show, nor does it throw its weight around or walk on other people's toes. Courtesy steps softly, speaks gently, showing honor and regard to all. For courtesy is love in action, and love will last forever.

God's Word on Etiquette, Manners, and Courtesy

Review these principles and share the scriptures. Have the girls take turns reading the verses aloud. (They are included in their workbooks.)

❀ Polite manners show honor and respect for others.

> *Be devoted to one another in brotherly love. Honor one another above yourselves* (Romans 12:10).

❀ Courteous manners show concern for the feelings of others.

> *Love does no harm to its neighbor. Therefore love is the fulfillment of the law* (Romans 13:10).

❀ Pleasant manners show kindness to others.

> *Be kind and compassionate to one another, forgiving each other, just as Christ forgave you* (Ephesians 4:32).

❀ Considerate, thoughtful manners fulfill the Golden Rule.

> *So in everything, do to others what you would have them do to you* (Matthew 7:12).

❀ Loving and gentle manners show the fruit of the Spirit.

> *The fruit of the Spirit is love, joy, peace, patience, kindness, goodness, faithfulness, gentleness and self control* (Galatians 5:22-23).

 *Write from Your Heart*

Go over the questions in the student workbook. You can have the girls answer them at home and discuss them briefly at the beginning of the next class if you'd like.

11

Confident Communication
Honoring Christ While Communicating

Purpose

To teach communication etiquette.

Prayer

Dear loving Father, thank You for speaking to me through Your Word. I pray for Your wisdom as I teach my girls how to honor You as they communicate with people. In Jesus' name. Amen.

Ponder

"Pleasant words are a honeycomb, sweet to the soul and healing to the bones" (Proverbs 16:24).

Preparation

✿ 2 cell phones for role-playing

✿ tube of toothpaste

✿ small plate or saucer

✿ paper towels (damp and dry)

✿ ask two girls to role-play this week's girls.

Tacky Tori doesn't make eye contact when talking to someone. She rudely interrupts other people's conversations to share her own point of view or to change the subject. She talks loudly on her cell phone no matter where she is, interfering with the conversations of others and revealing personal information.

Tactful Toni makes eye contact when talking with someone and uses a pleasant, quiet voice. She is polite and gracious in a group and waits her turn or gently signals she has something to say so she gets her turn. She hangs up her cell phone when she meets and visits people. She is careful not to have long phone conversations in public places.

Getting Started

"Hi, Girls! Welcome to class. Are you ready to get started? Let's begin with prayer."

Pray for the class and for your teaching.

"Who would like to recite memory verse Colossians 3:24?"

Whatever you do, work at it with all your heart, as working for the Lord, not for men, since you know that you will receive an inheritance from the Lord as a reward. It is the Lord Christ you are serving.

"Who would like to recite memory verse Philippians 4:13?"

I can do everything through him who gives me strength.

"Wonderful!
"So far we've learned about etiquette in terms of how we act and what we do in social situations. We've discovered that people decide a lot about us by what they see us do. Today we're going to shift our focus and explore how we can communicate effectively and honor Christ in every personal exchange. Words are powerful, and we want to use them wisely.
"Let me introduce you to *Tacky Tori* and *Tactful Toni*."

Have the girls come in and role-play, exaggerating the characteristics of each girl. Discuss how different the girls are and what makes each one bad or good communicators.

"*Tacky Tori* doesn't make eye contact when talking to someone, she rudely interrupts other people's conversations to share her own point of view or to change the subject, and she talks loudly on her cell phone no matter where she is, interfering with the conversations of others and revealing personal information in stores.

"*Tactful Toni* makes eye contact when talking with someone and uses a pleasant, quiet voice. She is polite and gracious in a group and waits her turn or gently signals she has something to say so she gets her turn. She hangs up her cell phone when she meets and visits people, and she is careful not to have long phone conversations in public places.

"We can bless or hurt people with our words. We can offer comfort or push people away. Words can build or break relationships."

Tech Etiquette 101

"To communicate well in today's world, we need to practice tech etiquette or 'Netiquette.' Communication forms have altered dramatically over the years. Today we have iPhones, BlackBerries, texting, Twitter, Facebook, MySpace, and more. And tomorrow there will be even more amazing communication choices. But the words we choose and the basics of communication haven't changed.

"Most people love to communicate. We enjoy connecting with each other; in fact, we need to connect. And kindness, politeness, and good manners facilitate positive communication and experiences. So what are some of the do's and don'ts in communication? Let's begin with cell phones."

Cell Phones

"One of the main problems with cell phones is that people get into their own world when they use them. When that little handheld gem rings, people drop everything to answer and totally tune out what they were doing or who they were with.

"When you choose to talk on the phone when you're with people, you're telling them they aren't very important.

"And when you talk on the phone in a restaurant or a store, the people around you aren't interested in your conversation but are forced to listen because of your proximity. And usually people raise their voices when talking on cells, so your conversation interrupts the conversations of those around you. You also might inadvertently reveal personal information about you or the person you're talking to. You might not want the whole school to know who you've got a crush on or what the doctor said…and neither may your friend.

"Be wise and be careful. Cell phones are great tools and have brought people closer together. In your workbook, look at the 10 things to remember when using a cell phone. How many of these do you practice? Do any of them seem scary or impossible?"

You may want to go through each item and discuss what the girls think and if they believe they'll be hard to implement.

❀ Just because it rings doesn't mean you have to answer it.

❀ When you're with someone else, don't answer your phone…or stay on it for more than a few seconds.

❀ Don't talk loudly. For an unknown reason, people seem to talk extra loud when they're on cells.

❀ Avoid annoying ring tones.

❀ Dis the disTones (ringtones and message with inappropriate noises and responses).

❀ Set a sweet tone.

❀ Use phone cameras for fun.

❀ Use your phone in appropriate places.

❀ Set your phone down or hang up when someone is serving you.

❀ Be grateful you have friends and family to talk to.

Texting

"Texting is fast and popular. Being able to get a quick answer from a friend without a lengthy conversation is great. Texting is also quiet and mostly unobtrusive, so it's a great alternative to a cell phone conversation when you're in a restaurant, crowded space, or public area."

Discussion "When have you used texting to avoid talking to someone face-to-face?"

"Have you ever used texting when you could have talked to the person just as easily? If so, why did you choose to text instead of call or go see your friend in person?"

"What drawbacks are there to texting?"

Note: These bulleted items are in the text of the student workbook.

❀ Texting leaves out body language, voice intonation, and other nuances and clues that help us correctly decipher messages and meanings.

❀ Texting can sound demanding or harsh because words are kept to a minimum.

❀ Texting opens up opportunities for cheating on tests at school.

❀ Texting inhibits close, deep friendships because emotions are hard to send and aren't face-to-face meetings.

❀ Texting can keep users from developing effective communication skills used in the "real world": writing, speaking, confidence in interpersonal relationships, reading body language.

"What are the positives about texting?"

Here are some positives to share.

❀ quick and easy communication

❀ communication is more frequent

❀ fast way to send an encouragement

❀ good way to remind people of meetings and homework

Instant Messaging

 "Communication always includes being thoughtful and kind. With today's quick communication technology, sometimes we hit Send before we've really thought about what we've said and how we said it.

"I've heard quite a few horror stories about inadvertently sending messages to the wrong people, too much personal information being shared that gets into public domain, and embarrassing typos and other goofs. Have you ever regretted sending a text? Has any message you've created ever gone to the wrong person?"

You might want to share an embarrassing story or two of your own to get the discussion started. This might also lead in to a reminder not to say anything negative about anyone to anyone.

"Let's go over the IM tips in your workbook."

The list in the student workbook goes into more detail.

- ✿ Ask before you start communicating.
- ✿ Respect each other's time.
- ✿ Be careful when picking a screen name.
- ✿ Be yourself.
- ✿ Think before you type.
- ✿ Don't write too much or too little.
- ✿ Guard against excluding or hurting someone.
- ✿ Use emoticons for clarification.
- ✿ Avoid conflict resolution in IM mode.
- ✿ Watch your time.

"IM is a great tool, but don't forget that 'face time' is important to relationships too."

Email

"Email is another form of communication, but it can be more thorough and detailed than some other forms of instant communication. Here are a few quick tips:

- ✿ Don't forward chain emails.
- ✿ Treat email like a letter.
- ✿ Use ecards to bless someone.

"Email is great for keeping in touch with your parents and for sending longer, personal messages."

Cyber-bullying

Cyber-bullying is such a critical concept and issue today that we suggest covering this area thoroughly. Mention how devastating cyber-bullying can be to teens. Note that it may even be illegal if someone's character or reputation is harmed.

This is also a great time to reiterate that sending suggestive stories or photos of anyone (themselves included) electronically is *never* a good idea. Even if they've been going with a boy for a long time, never send suggestive letters, notes, photographs, or illustrations. These inevitably get into the public domain and cause much grief.

"Electronic communication makes it so easy to casually send something that someone else could interpret negatively or get upset about. Without voice intonation and body language, people don't always get the full message…and since we don't see the other person, we don't always know how he or she interpreted our message or realize we need to clarify something.

"Like regular bullying, cyber-bullying can have degrees and can even occur unintentionally. Let's review the tips to avoid accidentally upsetting anyone."

Note: These are in the student workbook.

- ✿ Refuse to gossip or say anything negative.

- ✿ Avoid sending rude, inappropriate, or hurtful messages. Delete any you receive.

- ✿ Never post pictures of anyone—yourself included—on any site or electronic device. Don't send suggestive text or revealing photos to anyone.

- ✿ Impersonating someone else or using someone else's identity is illegal.

- ✿ Keep messages upbeat. Avoid teasing, harassing, and embarrassing someone.

- ✿ Use your own passwords.

- ✿ Don't click on any links or visit websites that are inappropriate. Besides filling your mind with garbage, even one click can allow massive amounts of spam, cookies, and viruses to be sent to your device for months and months.

- ✿ Be pleasant in chat rooms, IMs, game rooms, and so forth. You're representing Christ.

- ✿ Use communication tools to *connect* with others.

- ✿ Be a cyber-saint who represents Christ.

Reflecting Christ

"Techno gadgets are a lot of fun and make communication enjoyable. Let's make sure *we* stay in control…not the technology. It may sound scary, but we can turn off our electronics once in a while. Seldom do we get life-changing messages that need an immediate response. And when we do communicate, why not make sure we're uplifting and encouraging people? In today's world, people don't hear enough positive news or compliments."

Discussion Ask for two volunteers to come up to the front of the class. Squeeze a significant amount of toothpaste onto a plate. Then ask the girls to put it back in. (Have paper towels handy for cleanup.)

"What do you think trying to put toothpaste back into the tube tells us about communication?"

"That's right. Once we've said or sent words, we can't take them back. So it's vital that we think about what we say and how we say it *before* we hit Send. Psalm 19:14 says, '*May the words of my mouth and the meditation of my heart be pleasing in your sight, O LORD, my Rock and my Redeemer.'* What a wonderful verse for us to memorize and follow. And how do we get to where our communication is always uplifting and positive and godly? By reading and studying God's Word, talking with Jesus, and spending time with Christians.

"How often do you meet with Jesus in a time of meditation, sweet communion, and listening?"

"With your busy schedules, spending time every day in prayer and Bible study may seem difficult—even impossible. But the benefits will amaze you! Why not set a time to meet with Jesus every day for the next week? Begin small—5 minutes at first will get you started. Gradually build up to 15 minutes. Soon you'll want to spend even more time with your Lord and in studying the Bible. You'll experience a spiritual and personal growth spurt.

"God wants to meet with you every day. He wants to hear about your dreams, your goals, your problems, your rejoicings. And He wants to communicate with you through His Word and through His Holy Spirit."

Share ideas with the girls on how they can structure a quiet time. You may want to bring in a pretty basket with a Bible, notepad, pens, prayer journal, book of meditations, and other items that might help in communing with God.

Write from Your Heart

Go over the questions in the student workbook. You can have the girls answer them at home and discuss them briefly at the beginning of the next class if you'd like.

Remind the girls to memorize Psalm 19:14 so they can say it from their hearts at the next class.

12

Taming Your Tongue
Guarding Against Gossip

Purpose

To guide the girls in understanding the tongue has power of life and death—and the importance of putting a guard at the gate of our mouths.

Prayer

Gracious God, thank You for creating us with the desire to communicate with You and with each other. Give me the words to help my girls understand the harm careless words can cause. Amen.

Ponder

"Set a guard over my mouth, O Lord; keep watch over the door of my lips" (Psalm 141:3).

Preparation

❀ bring 4 "gifts" to illustrate the closing lesson:

- stinky trash
- something gooey and messy and sloppy wrapped in old newspaper
- an empty gold foil box with lid adorned with gold ribbon

- clear, see-through bag with toiletry items that look pretty and smell great. If you choose, you can bring enough to pass out one item to each girl as a reminder to keep their speech encouraging

✿ a sheet to cover the "gifts" until ready to share them

Getting Started

"Today we're going to talk about a problem that affects every person on the planet. One of the most powerful human forces for good and evil is our tongues…the words we speak. Before we dive in, let's pray."

Pray for your girls and your teaching.

"Let's review memory verse Colossians 3:12-14. Who would like to recite it for us first?"

Therefore, as God's chosen people, holy and dearly loved, clothe yourselves with compassion, kindness, humility, gentleness and patience. Bear with each other and forgive whatever grievances you may have against one another. Forgive as the Lord forgave you. And over all these virtues put on love, which binds them all together in perfect unity.

"Anyone else want to try it?"

"How many of you know girls like *Gossiping Gertrude?* She changes 'best friends' every day. She flits from one person to the next, never creating lasting relationships. Gossiping Gertrude is a 'fair weather' friend. When times get tough, she moves on. Unfortunately, she shares those tough times…and anything else 'interesting'…with everyone. Her conversations are peppered with mild swear words to garner interest and create a stir.

"And then there's her counterpart, *Faithful Francesca.* She's kind to everyone she meets. She has a few very good friends she hangs with regularly. She keeps their confidences and supports and encourages them in their activities. She always has something positive to say and often compliments people and points out their good points to others.

"Now, take a second to think about you and your friends. Who do you and your friends resemble the most—Gossiping Gertrude or Faithful Francesca?"

[Pause.]

"When we look at them side by side, it's easy to see which person is the 'best' one to be and know, but, realistically, we all have moments where we're both of these girls, don't we? But we don't have to be a Gossiping Gertrude. We can leave her behind. How? By studying and knowing God's Word. Matthew 12:34 says, '*Out of the overflow of the heart the mouth speaks.*'

"Okay, let's open our Bibles to Proverbs 10:19 and read it together: *'When words are many, sin is not absent, but he who holds his tongue is wise.'* We've all said things we've regretted. What have you said that you wish you hadn't? What were the results, and how did you resolve the situation?"

"God's Word has much to say about our tongues. Proverbs 12:18 says, *'The tongue has the power of life and death.'* Does this verse seem extreme? Think about how devastating and long-lasting words can be. Most of us have been told something that hurt us. And even though the people may have apologized or we realized the words weren't true, the pain lingered in our hearts. Words can wound our spirits deeply.

"How are your words? What do people learn from your speech?"

"Some people look very nice on the outside, but when they open their mouths venom sprays on everyone they meet. They love to stir up gossip and cause dissension. How do you define gossip?"

"Unfortunately, we've all gossiped more than once. A gossip is 'a person who habitually reveals personal or sensational facts about others.' Gossipers take the saying, 'It doesn't have to be true to be interesting' to a new level. They create waves of hurt that last a long time and damage hearts and reputations. Even though we often joke about gossip, the truth is that our words have the power to crush someone's spirit.

"Often gossip comes wrapped in good intentions: 'I'd like the group to pray for Theodora today because her boyfriend went out on her, and she doesn't know what to do.' And when was the last time you heard someone say, 'Don't tell anyone but...'?

"Gossip can seem exciting and even harmless, but it's not. And once gossip starts, it's almost impossible to stop it or end it. It spreads like wildfire—out of control, jumping from one person to another, often gaining in intensity.

"So how can we put a halt to gossiping? The first thing is to realize it begins with us. With you and me. When we hear gossip, we need to *not* pass it on. In fact, we can even tell the person sharing that we don't listen to negative or titillating details about someone else. And by doing this in a nice and respectful way, we can share that we're not gossiping because we believe in God and follow His principles in the Bible.

"And, of course, if we do hear gossip, the important thing is not to pass it on. Why don't you and your friends set up a code word to help you avoid gossiping? If one of you hears gossip or starts to share gossip, a person could say the code word as a gentle reminder. Philippians 4:8 is a great reference. You could use '4:8' as your code: *'Finally, [sisters], whatever is true, whatever is noble, whatever is right, whatever is pure, whatever is lovely, whatever is admirable—if anything is excellent or praiseworthy—think about such things.'*

"Did you notice what we did? We used the powerful Word of God to extinguish a spark that could turn into a gossip wildfire. James said no one can tame the tongue, but we can work toward being godly in our speech."

Note: The girls are asked to write the following information in their workbooks.

"What are some tips to controlling speech?

- ✿ Ask God to put a 'guard over your mouth' so only edifying words come out (Psalm 141:3).

- ✿ Ask a friend to hold you accountable.

- ✿ Put scripture verses about watching your tongue in strategic places, such as by the phone, to remind you not to gossip.

- ✿ Study God's Word and spend time with God so your mind is continually being renewed (Romans 12:2).

"The next idea is to evaluate how we treat the people around us. Are we kind? Do we include everyone? Are we helpful? One way teen girls may inadvertently participate in gossip is by becoming part of a 'select' group of girls. Cliques start innocently enough as girls with common interests gather, but often they become exclusive. Does your group exclude other girls? Do the other girls in your group reach out and invite others to join in activities? Unfortunately exclusive cliques often become havens for gossipers. Some girls even spread rumors and talk trash about the 'wannabees.'

"Girls, cliques can be a big problem in school and even wield social power. No one likes to be excluded. God loves all of us. He invites *every* person to accept His love and be part of His family. Let's follow His lead!

"Another great solution for curbing gossip is to share something encouraging about someone instead of passing on 'dirt.' "

 You can have the girls take turns reading the positive Bible verses about the tongue. They're printed below and in the student workbook for reference.

My heart is glad and my tongue rejoices (Psalm 16:9).

My tongue will speak of your righteousness and of your praises all day long (Psalm 35:28).

The tongue of the righteous is choice silver (Proverbs 10:20).

At the name of Jesus every knee should bow, in heaven and on earth and under the earth, and every tongue confess that Jesus Christ is Lord, to the glory of God the Father (Philippians 2:10-11).

Judas and Silas, who themselves were prophets, said much to encourage and strengthen the brothers (Acts 15:32).

After that, we who are still alive and are left will be caught up together with them in the clouds to meet the Lord in the air. And so we will be with the Lord forever. Therefore encourage each other with these words (1 Thessalonians 4:17-18).

"Words can be used to encourage, energize, and empower. Our goal is to be kind and loving so we can tell people that our loving heavenly Father cares about them too. Have you noticed how you feel when you've received praise and recognition? Why not help others get that same lift by sharing a sincere compliment or good word? Their eyes will light up and they will be energized.

"And like gossip, encouragement can spread like wildfire…but this time creating heat that warms hearts and heals wounds. When we encourage people, they feel better about themselves and, in turn, say something positive to others. These people feel better and pass on their good attitude to the people they encounter. The more we practice doing this, the more it becomes second nature to be upbeat. We can encourage hearts and build confidence in those around us. Hebrews 3:13 says, *'Encourage one another daily.'* First Thessalonians 5:11 says, *'Encourage one another and build each other up.'*

"Think of encouragement as filling up someone's gas tank with confidence and energy. Let's face it, we all need to be encouraged. When we feel encouraged, we do feel energized and empowered to keep on keeping on.

 Discussion

"What are some encouraging words people have said to you?"

"How did they make you feel?"

"What words can you use to encourage people this week?"

"And, girls, don't forget that even brothers and sisters can use some positive encouragement from you. And why not let your moms and dads know how much you appreciate them?"

Four Gifts

Note: This section is not in the student workbook.

 Discussion

"I brought some gifts to share today."

Pull out the first gift: stinky trash.

"Oh oh. This is really smelly and yucky. I don't suppose any of you want to take this home? What do you think this present represents when it comes to gossip?"

Meaning: The ugly, nasty words of gossip are hurtful and spread hate. Note that the stink remains for a long time.

"Girls, I don't like this gift either. Let's get rid of it! I'm sure the next gift will be better."

Pull out the second gift: something gooey and messy and sloppy wrapped in old newspaper.

"Well, at least this present isn't stinky. What do you think this package is saying about gossip?"

Meaning: How our careless and sloppy word choices inadvertently hurt someone's feelings or spread gossip. We don't intend to be mean; we just don't think through what we say. Our tongues aren't reflecting hearts filled with the Holy Spirit.

> "You know, I don't like this present either. Will one of you take it home? No? Well, let's toss it in the garbage then. Surely the next present will be better."

Pull out the third gift: an empty gold foil box with lid adorned with gold ribbon.

> "Yes, this seems much better. It's pretty and nice. Let's open it up. Oh! It's empty? What could this represent when it comes to gossip?"

Meaning: People flatter us with pretty words, but they aren't sincere or true. They want something or are being catty. It also represents us when we offer insincere compliments. Compliments offered without real caring are empty and worthless.

> "This present *looked like a good gift,* but it wasn't really. The outside and inside didn't match. Let's get rid of it too. Surely the next present will be good."

Pull out the fourth gift: a clear, see-through bag with toiletry items that look pretty and smell great.

> "Finally! A real gift. We can tell instantly that what's inside is beautiful and smells wonderful. What does this represent when it comes to our tongues?"

Meaning: We want our words to be sweet and gracious, imbued with the delightful *fragrance* of Christ.

> "Second Corinthians 2:14-15 says, '*Thanks be to God, who always leads us in triumphal procession in Christ and through us spreads everywhere the fragrance of the knowledge of him. For we are to God the aroma of Christ among those who are being saved.*'"

If you brought enough gift items to share, give one to each girl in the class.

Reflecting Christ

> "As Christians, the Holy Spirit lives within us. When we focus on Him and live for Jesus, we draw on God's love and strength. Proverbs 16:24 says, '*Pleasant words are a honeycomb, sweet to the soul and healing to the bones.*' Let's draw people to our Lord through our sincere care for them."

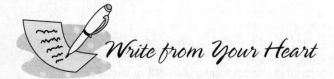

Write from Your Heart

Ask the girls what verses in this chapter spoke to their hearts. Let them share how they'll apply the wisdom in that verse to their lives.

You can go over the other questions in the student workbook or have the girls answer them at home and discuss them briefly at the beginning of the next class.

13

Caring Enough to Confront
Handling Conflicts Biblically

Purpose

To give girls biblical principles and practical strategies to resolve conflicts.

Prayer

Loving Father, please give me Your wisdom as I teach these girls how to handle conflict Your way. Speaking the truth in love requires tact and finesse. Help me explain this clearly. Amen.

Ponder

"Let us therefore make every effort to do what leads to peace and to mutual edification" (Romans 14:19).

Preparation

❀ whiteboard or chalkboard and writing implements

❀ 3 "conflicts scenarios" written on notecards for the girls to resolve in groups (see "What Would You Do?" section)

Getting Started

"Hi, girls! Welcome back to class. We have something very important to cover today, so let's get started by praying."

Pray for the girls to have open hearts and minds as they learn about conflicts and how to handle them God's way.

"We all encounter conflicts so it's vital that we discover how to handle them in ways that are positive, workable, and end in honoring our Lord. God provides valuable instructions on resolving conflicts in His Word. Who will read Matthew 18, verses 15 through 17, for us?"

If your brother sins against you, go and show him his fault, just between the two of you. If he listens to you, you have won your brother over. But if he will not listen, take one or two others along, so that "every matter may be established by the testimony of two or three witnesses." If he refuses to listen to them, tell it to the church; and if he refuses to listen even to the church, treat him as you would a pagan or a tax collector.

"I'm sure you've experienced conflicts in some of your relationships. What types of conflicts do you and your friends encounter? For instance, has a friend ever asked you to do something you thought wasn't right? Have you gotten into disagreements with family members? Without naming names or getting too detailed, let's make a list of some of the conflicts we've experienced."

Write the conflicts the girls share on a whiteboard or chalkboard.

"I'm sure many of these conflicts were resolved just fine, but some may have stuck around and the effects still linger today. Let's look at two girls and how they handle conflict.

"*Anastasia* panics when a problem arises. She gets anxious and escapes the situation by going to her room or any place she can be alone. Then she paces the floor, bites her fingernails, and worries out loud about what's going to happen. She blames the other people, and wonders why they're so unreasonable. She hopes the problem will just disappear. But we know that doesn't usually happen, don't we? Although some minor ones may, most won't. *Avoider Anastasia* doesn't do anything to resolve the problem, so it festers and gets worse, making her relationships with the people involved awkward and tense.

"*Rosaline*, however, knows a problem usually won't get resolved on its own. She actively seeks God's wisdom and asks for His help in the situation. She evaluates her involvement to see if she did anything to make the situation escalate into a conflict. If she did, she asks God and the people involved for forgiveness. She also speaks the truth in love and extends God's grace and mercy to the people involved. *Resolving Rosaline* continues to be positive in her interactions and encourages the participants to work through the situation.

"Take a minute to think about the last conflict you were involved in. Did you resemble Avoider Anastasia or Resolver Rosaline?"

"No one likes conflicts, but they occur. Esther 1:18 says, '*There will be no end of disrespect and discord.*' Remember the principles we read about in Matthew 18?

❀ Deal with the people involved in the conflict directly and face-to-face if possible.

❀ If the situation doesn't resolve, ask one or two people who are objective, calm, and wise to go with you to talk to the people again.

❀ If the situation still doesn't get resolved, go to your church leadership, explain the situation, and seek their counsel.

"This sounds pretty straightforward, doesn't it? But that doesn't mean it will always be easy. Today we're going to discover how to handle conflict resolution by focusing on biblical principles, looking at some practical strategies, exploring how to resolve and reconcile, and understanding and offering forgiveness. As Proverbs 19:20 points out: '*Listen to advice and accept instruction, and in the end you will be wise.*'"

Conflict Resolution 101

"*Conflicts* are 'disagreements, struggles, or battles when two or more people have different viewpoints and/or approaches in a situation or event.'

"Picture a girl walking into a room full of people having a good time. Let's call her Helena. Suddenly the room gets quiet, and almost everyone turns to stare at her. Feeling awkward, she moves close to her best friend and asks what's going on. Her friend replies that she heard from a friend, who heard it from Harriet, that Helena had cheated on today's math test.

"Knowing she didn't, Helena is shocked and angry.

"What will Helena do? Hopefully she'll remember 'honey attracts and vinegar repels.' In other words, if she wants to attract Harriet's good will to work out the problem, she needs to approach her sweetly. Approaching her with anger or irritation will sour (vinegar) the air and inhibit resolution.

"In Matthew 18, verses 15 through 18, Jesus provides specific instructions for handling disagreements. The first step is approaching the person or persons we're dealing with and addressing the problem to come to a resolution. Since 'problem' starts with a 'p,' let's use that letter as a starting point.

"First, *pray*. Ask Jesus to give you wisdom, a gentle attitude for conciliation, and the best words for communicating your concern and desire to reach a resolution.

"Next *propose* a time and place to meet privately.

"*Prepare* before you ask for the meeting by using the 'sandwich' method. This is starting and ending with something positive and putting what you want to work on in the middle. This is a great communication principle that works in a multitude of situations:

✿ For instance, you can ask the person you're meeting with to join you in prayer.

✿ After the prayer share something you like about that person, perhaps how much you admire his or her flexibility, reasoning abilities, upbeat attitude.

✿ Then state the issue simply and clearly. Don't be accusatory or combative. Keep a cool head and own the problem by using 'I' statements: 'I'm concerned because I heard you were saying some negative things about me. Is this true? Have I done something to offend you? If I have, let's talk about it.'

✿ At the end offer or negotiate a *proactive* plan on how to avoid this type of problem in the future.

✿ The last thing you want to do is assure the person that you will keep your conversation confidential. You'll *protect* the person's privacy and your own. Don't post anything about the conversation electronically or share personal details about the discussion that may make the other person feel uncomfortable or put him or her in a bad light.

"So remember: *pray*, *propose* a time to meet, *prepare* for the meeting, develop a *proactive* plan, and *protect* the reputation of everyone involved."

Face Time

"In our fast-paced world, it's so easy to contact someone electronically. But conflicts are much easier to resolve in person. Electronic communication…and even telephone conversations… don't allow us to pick up on subtle clues on what the other person is thinking or feeling, how well he or she is understanding us, and how our message is being interpreted. Remember that our goal is to '*encourage one another and build each other up*' (1 Thessalonians 5:11)."

What Would You Do? (This is not in the student workbook.)

Divide into groups. Hand each group a "conflict card" you've prepared. Let them role-play to resolve the conflicts. Here are some possible scenarios:

✿ You brought your new jacket to the football game and left it on the bleachers. On Monday, you see a student wearing a coat just like yours. In fact, it even has a tiny spot of grease from where you brushed against something in the garage. You're certain it's your jacket. What will you do?

✿ While you were taking a class you noticed the girl next to you texting someone. You saw her read a message and then write something on her test paper. You suspect she was cheating. Later you overhear her talking to a friend, "Thanks for texting the answers. I didn't have time to study for the stupid test." What will you do?

✿ You've just been invited to a party Friday night. No parents are going to be there, and you just heard some boys talk about spiking the drinks and bringing some "happy pills" to jazz up the party. Your best friend is excited about the get-together and tells you someone you've been secretly admiring is going to be there. What will you do?

Reflecting Christ

"We've been talking about biblical and practical ways to work through conflicts. But what happens when you've been offended and you're still upset? What if *you* don't want to forgive the other person or work out the problem? What if the person hurt you deeply by stealing something you value, going out with your boyfriend, or saying something horrible about you behind your back?

"As Christians, we are called to forgive. Colossians 3:13 says, *'Bear with each other and forgive whatever grievances you may have against one another. Forgive as the Lord forgave you.'* That's pretty clear. It won't always be easy. How do you change your heart? You study God's Word and talk to Jesus about the situation. You can also get advice from someone you admire and respect who knows Jesus and studies His Word.

"Forgiveness is not the same as reconciliation. Forgiveness is about what was done to you, and reconciliation is focused on healing the relationship or resolving a specific problem. You can forgive someone without having a close relationship with the person. Forgiveness is an act of your will based on your faith in Christ Jesus. June Hunt wrote an excellent book called *How to Forgive When You Don't Feel Like It*. She points out that forgiveness…

✿ opens the door to God's forgiveness

✿ prevents bitterness

✿ closes a door to Satan in our lives

✿ brings us into the light of Christ

✿ leads to blessings for the other person and us

"But what if you're the person at fault? What if you did something that caused pain or discomfort? When you realize what you've done, talk to God, ask for His forgiveness, and then go to the person involved and ask for his or her forgiveness. *'Confess your sins to each other and pray for each other so that you may be healed'* (James 5:16). And what do you do if the person refuses to forgive you? You say, 'Thank you for hearing me out. I'll continue to pray about this situation. I'm really sorry for the pain I caused you.' And then you move on with your life. Some people need time to adjust to the situation and work through the issues. However, you do follow through and pray. The last part of James 5:16 says, *'The prayer of a righteous man is powerful and effective.'*"

A Final Thought

"Relationships are exciting, fulfilling, and absolutely necessary to our well-being. But they also include disagreements, misunderstandings, and opportunities that cause us to grow spiritually, emotionally, and mentally. Here are some great scriptures from the book of Matthew. Let's look at them and read them together. Write down their addresses so you'll have them for the times you need encouragement as you deal with conflicts."

Have the girls take turns reading these verses.

You have heard that it was said, "Love your neighbor and hate your enemy." But I tell you: Love your enemies and pray for those who persecute you (Matthew 5:43-44).

If you are offering your gift at the altar and there remember that your brother has something against you, leave your gift there in front of the altar. First go and be reconciled to your brother; then come and offer your gift (Matthew 5:23-24).

You have heard that it was said, "Eye for eye, and tooth for tooth." But I tell you, Do not resist an evil person. If someone strikes you on the right cheek, turn to him the other also (Matthew 5:38-39).

If someone wants to sue you and take your tunic, let him have your cloak as well. If someone forces you to go one mile, go with him two miles (Matthew 5:40-41).

"God's wisdom is awesome and His power and grace are ever powerful. When problems arise and you are struggling, turn to Him. He will give you the strength to work through the conflict. He will give you the grace to forgive and move on. What a wonderful heavenly Father we have!"

Write from Your Heart

If you'd like, you can go through the "Write from Your Heart" questions with your girls or have them answer them at home.

A Time to Celebrate!

Dear Teachers,

Congratulations on teaching the *New Christian Charm Course*. We appreciate your hard work and effort to help girls grow strong spiritually, mentally, socially, emotionally, and physically. It's hard to see this wonderful time with your girls come to a close, isn't it?

We suggest you hold a special "closing" event to celebrate your girls and thank them for going on this journey. We offer the following suggestions to help get your creative juices flowing.

A Festive Dinner

Hold a dinner party at your home or decorate the classroom for a festive, special evening. You can have it catered, fix the food yourself, have the girls help you, or enlist the help of some of your friends or the parents of the girls.

If you'd like, you can tell each girl they can bring their mom or a special woman friend if their mom can't come. Tell the girls ahead of time that each one will share some highlights of what they learned in the course. To make sure everything is covered, you can have the girls volunteer for certain areas or even put the topics in a hat and have them draw their topics.

Let the girls plan the sharing entertainment and help organize the dinner. They'll be more involved that way. This gives them a great opportunity to practice their new skills.

A Slumber Party

Have a wonderful "Girl's Night Out" at your house or in the classroom. Let the girls plan the activities, but suggest they include healthy food, manicure and pedicure time, and makeup makeovers.

Allow time for Bible study, prayer, and sharing how God is working in the girls' lives. Then open the time to general talk about what's happening in their lives. We've found that girls really open up and share their hearts. Remind the girls that what is said during the evening is confidential and private.

A Scrapbook Party

Gather the materials for scrapbooking and have an energetic evening of creating scrapbook pages of what's happening in their lives and what they've learned in the *New Christian Charm Course*. You can prepare Scripture printouts in fun fonts, various graphics, many colors and patterns of paper, and so forth. Invite the girls to bring any scrapbooking materials they may have.

You can also make this event more focused by having the girls create their charm course "to do" charts. Have copies of the chart in chapter 9 of this book available for reference. The girls can decorate the poster for their bedroom with Scripture verses, flowers, hearts, and so forth. They can even have their friends autograph the charts for permanent keepsakes.

In preplanning, have the girls volunteer to bring healthy snacks. You can also encourage donating $5 each to cover the cost of scrapbook supplies. In your church or circle of friends you may discover someone who has a lot of die cuts and specialty scissors. Invite them to come and share their "know how" and equipment. Or you can invite a professional scrapbook person, such as someone from "Creative Memories." However, that usually entails a sales pitch of some kind, which you'll want to tone down or avoid altogether.

Mother/Daughter Retreat

This is truly a wonderful event! You can plan lots of teaching and sharing opportunities that highlight Christian charm. Create "generational giggles" by having the moms share some of their foibles when it comes to etiquette and learning about manners.

Include time for giving each other manicures, eating healthy snacks, having a short Bible study, and sharing prayer requests.

Spa Time

Set up a spa at your house or in the classroom. Have each girl bring supplies for washing hair, doing nails, and putting on makeup. Let the girls know that you'll also have extra supplies in case some of the girls forget or don't have what they'd like to use. You can make this a "class event" only or invite the moms and special women guests.

More Suggestions and Ideas

We've put a special section for Christian charm teachers and girls on Jody's website, www. capehartconnection.com. You'll find more ideas for closing events, suggestions for keeping in contact with "your" girls via special lunch meetings, Bible studies, prayer times, and more.

In updating Emily Hunter's *Christian Charm Course*, some material had to be left out, so some of that is on Jody's website. You'll also find expanded information on a variety of topics.

Thank you again for sharing your time, love, prayers, and energy with the girls in your class. We have so much to offer as we help these lovely girls grow into healthy young women. We appreciate your heart for God's girls.

If you'd like to contact us, please write to:

Jody Capehart
Hope for the Heart
PO Box 7
Dallas, TX 75221

You can also check out at: www.capehartconnection.com

In the love of our Lord and Savior,
Emily, Jody, Angela, and Amy

Personal Notes

Personal Notes

Personal Notes